MALLMANN ON FIRE

Also by Francis Mallmann
Seven Fires

MALLMANN ON FIRE

FRANCIS MALLMANN

with Peter Kaminsky and Donna Gelb

PRINCIPAL PHOTOGRAPHY BY SANTIAGO SOTO MONLLOR

ARTISAN

Published by Artisan
A division of Workman Publishing Company, Inc.
225 Varick Street
New York, NY 10014-4381
artisanbooks.com

Published simultaneously in Canada by Thomas Allen &
Son, Limited.

Library of Congress Cataloging-in-Publication Data

Mallmann, Francis.
  Mallmann on fire / Francis Mallmann with Peter Kaminsky
and Donna Gelb.
    pages cm
  Includes index.
  ISBN 978-1-57965-537-2
  1. Cooking, Argentine. 2. Barbecuing. 3. Frying. 4.
Broiling. 5. Cooking—Patagonia (Argentina and Chile)
J. Kaminsky, Peter. II. Gelb, Donna. III. Title.
  TX716.A7M268 2014
  641.5982—dc23

                    2014004632

Design by Jan Derevjanik

Printed in China

10 9 8 7 6 5 4 3 2

Preceding: Mendoza at twilight with the vineyards
and the Andes in the distance.

Get Up and Get Out

Some years ago, it struck me how settled in our ways we have all become. Our evenings take us from the office to the couch, from the couch to the kitchen, from the kitchen to the easy chair by the television, and from the easy chair to bed. I realized that for most people, the mere thought of grabbing a basket packed with a picnic and thinking of an outdoor space to enjoy was just that . . . only a thought.

So I decided to make a TV show to prompt them out into the wild. It would be based on the simplest recipes, requiring barely any equipment. I began the first show by putting on my favorite tweed jacket, a hat, and some walking boots. I put a potato in my left pocket and a tin cup with two eggs in my right pocket, along with a metal spoon, salt, pepper, and a chunk of butter wrapped in paper. I held an onion in my hand and, instead of an Hermès handkerchief, I stuck a handful of fresh parsley in the top pocket of my jacket.

Then I walked into the hills until I got to a nicè stream, where I started piling up fallen branches to start my fire. From the streambed, I selected a large, flat gray stone with a slight hollow in the middle, just like a soup plate. I still remember looking through the clear

CONTENTS

ix   GET UP AND GET OUT

1   **ON TOP OF THE WORLD**
BY PETER KAMINSKY

7   **SOY PATAGÓN**

13   **MY FIRES**

21   Appetizers and Salads
55   **TRAVELS WITH FIRE**
PARIS, FRANCE

63   Light Meals
83   **TRAVELS WITH FIRE**
LA RUTA AZUL, PATAGONIA

91   Beef, Lamb, and Pork
102   ANYTIME, ANYWHERE
139   **TRAVELS WITH FIRE**
NEW YORK, NEW YORK

145   Birds
152   IN THE SNOW
161   **TRAVELS WITH FIRE**
GARZÓN, URUGUAY

 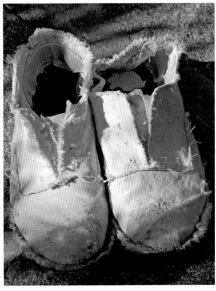 

169 Fish and Shellfish

207 Vegetables and Beans
233 **TRAVELS WITH FIRE**
TRANCOSO, BRAZIL

241 Desserts
246 TEXTILES

263 Country Breads
271 **TRAVELS WITH FIRE**
"THE ISLAND," PATAGONIA

279 Basics

292 **SOME IMPORTANT TOOLS**

295 **ACKNOWLEDGMENTS**

296 **INDEX**

ON TOP OF THE WORLD

BY PETER KAMINSKY

Francis Mallmann views food as he does almost everything else, as an aesthetic expression. So, yes, the dining is unforgettable, but to this native of Patagonia, food is the melody in a larger symphony of pleasure. Almost as important are the setting, the plates, the linens, the scenery, the music, and the books that he sometimes uses instead of place cards (this morning, my table on the patio of his small hotel in the village of Garzón was reserved with a volume of Rilke's poetry).

As I reflect on my twenty years in Mallmann Land—which my wife refers to as "The Realm of the Senses"—I'm sitting on a green hill overlooking a broad valley: a vista of forests, fields, vineyards, and olive groves. The warm breeze rising off the valley floor is soft and sweet.

Around my perch, a platoon of workers has been deployed—some with bright head scarves and tattoos that would not look out of place on a pirate frigate. They lug enormous iron implements and place them along the ridge. The shapes and rusty orange color call to mind the sculptures of Richard Serra.

This iron, though, is an expression of a different art—wood-fired cooking. There is a huge cauldron that will be filled with lard for frying empanadas stuffed with fatty beef, olives, and eggs, in the style of Salta, in the north of Argentina. It was in this province—peopled by Incas and the descendants of Canary Islanders—that Francis, in his twenties, first encountered the seven fires that would redefine the oeuvre of this classically trained chef and lead him to devote his career to restoring wood-fired cooking to a place of honor in the world of big-league cuisine.

In addition to the cauldron, there is a huge *chapa,* or *plancha,* that takes eight people to muscle into position. To its left, several men carry a *parrilla* unlike any barbecue grate I have ever seen. It looks like an old iron box spring as seen in a fun-house mirror, higher on one end and sloping down to shorter legs. Also, as at many of Francis's big productions, there is an *infiernillo*—literal translation, "little hell"—an Inca-inspired device of his own invention where a tray with a salt-crusted whole fish is sandwiched between two cast-iron platforms, each with its own roaring fire. In full blaze, it conjures up a brace of funeral pyres for a couple of fallen Vikings.

Farther up the hill, a ring of iron—four inches thick and five feet in diameter—is muscled into place. It is not a complete circle: one end is open so that the radiant heat of a bonfire can slowly cook two lambs that are placed on iron crosses about six feet from the circle of fire.

Overlooking all this iron, there are three wooden platforms of weathered timber. Tall pieces of lumber reach up from the corners of each platform, like the bedposts of a canopy bed. They serve no apparent purpose other than to mark off a space that, while it is completely open to the air, somehow feels enclosed.

Francis, in tattered jeans, white shirt with sleeves partly rolled, and sunglasses, sits at one of the tables, displaying a wide smile.

Looking again at the assemblage of wood and iron in the last rays of sunlight, I reflect that an archaeologist might be excused for thinking that he had come upon the ceremonial precinct of a past civilization.

We inch our way down the dirt road that leads back to town, a few miles away. Francis slows his four-wheel drive, ceding the right of way to a small viper retreating from the road. "She lives here," he says. "She's doing no harm." Then he cranks up the volume on the sound system to a thumping rock-and-roll level.

When we return the next day, the crew is busy preparing dinner for twenty, a modest size by Mallmann standards (I once assisted him on a phalanx of *infiernillos* as we baked nine huge salmon to feed three hundred people). On the *chapas,* smashed potatoes, basted in butter, crust over: as crunchy as a handful of potato chips on the outside and creamy within. The two iron crosses, now bearing trussed lambs, are angled away from the roaring fire. I can't help but think, just for a moment, that this is Calvary for the lambs, but as soon as I get a whiff of the meat, I banish my gray thought. I walk over to the "box spring," where four whole rib eyes are cooking, but when I put my hand out to gauge the heat, there is none. Well, almost none.

"I cook them for nine hours at the lowest heat," Francis explains. "Maybe 120 degrees. The meat will be rosy red all the way through . . . and juicy, but with a good crust."

Yesterday's band of stevedores now looks a little less like Jack Sparrow's crewmates, in their cook's uniforms: white aprons with a few colorful and delicate stripes running down the midline. The same pattern marks the white cloths that cover the dining tables set up on the wooden platforms. Both are designed by Francis; cloth, in all colors and patterns, is central to his aesthetic. In his constant travels, he shops for beautiful textiles. He keeps warehouses full of them wherever he works, using some for pillows, as throws over couches and chairs, as table coverings: damask from Syria, batik from Indonesia, antique bed linens from Belgian monasteries, vicuna shawls from the markets of San Telmo in Buenos Aires. He uses textiles to paint the scene whenever he creates an event, and every meal is an event. At this one, though, nature provides most of the color. The man-made accents are stark and chaste, a way to define a space that brings some—but not too much—order into nature.

The long refectory tables, oversize linen napkins, and long-stemmed wineglasses glinting in the sun provide a counterpoint to the rustic cookery. Francis celebrates contrast—between the raw and the burnt, between unruly nature and refined artifice. It is a tension that he always plays upon and that rarely fails to seduce his guests.

He welcomes tonight's group with cocktails made with limes and *cachaça,* the Brazilian distillate of sugarcane that packs a moonshine wallop. The guests bite into their empanadas, inevitably slurping the innards (there is no decorous way to eat one: you just commit and pray that you don't stain your shirt). Francis, now in a chef's coat, glides among them. He projects reserved friendliness. He is not a glad-hander. All his extroversion goes into making the moment—art-directing it as much as cheffing it.

He prods the beef, slices off a piece of lamb, and tastes it. If someone approaches and asks a question about the cooking method, he answers as he goes about checking the doneness of the food. He needs no digital probes, no knives to cut into the meat. He can tell by feel.

The party is seated, their platters heaped. No one, I think, can be expected to eat this much, but somehow they do. They are enraptured by the place, the aroma, the elegance of it all. The conversation sounds as mirthful and light as the tinkle of the wine goblets. Francis delivers a welcome speech and a toast. I want to say a "champagne toast," because it seems like a champagne moment, but I can't recall Francis ever drinking champagne. He is a man of very particular tastes.

His work done, he slips away from the diners and joins me on a bench. The sun has dipped below the hills, but the sky is still gold, with a blush of pink. He requests a favorite Van Morrison track on my iPhone—the haunting "On Hyndford Street." "Take me back, take me way, way, way back," Morrison sings. Francis listens intently. His gaze turns inward. He wraps his old camel-hair sweater (from Lisbon, 1992) around him against the evening chill. The sound of a chorus of birds, nature's evensong, ripples across the valley.

The party is seated, the
guests' platters heaped.
No one, I think, can be
expected to eat this much,
but somehow they do.

SOY PATAGÓN

I am an Argentine, with an Uruguayan
mother, and descended from European
immigrants. I have lived in Illinois and
California, on Long Island, and in Paris
and Italy. All of those places are part
of me, but I still see myself as a son of
one of the last remote corners of the
planet: Patagonia, bordered on the
west by the snowcapped peaks of the
Andes, glimmering glaciers, slumbering
volcanoes, and hundreds of lakes
and rivers, which flow east into grassy
pampas and deserts and then to the
windswept shores of the southern
Atlantic Ocean. Patagonia, where the

mainland tapers like an arrowhead until it ends at the Straits of Magellan; just across those straits is Tierra del Fuego, the Land of Fire.

Patagonia is an immense and beautiful land. Mountains, deserts, and coast: we have them all. Of the three, I would say my heart is in the mountains and their lakes. It's where I was raised, in the town of Bariloche—now a glamorous tourist destination, but in my childhood, a much smaller mountain town. I understand the winds there, the sun, the storms, the clouds. Because I grew up there, I can read the language of its geography. One glance to the west, where the storms come from, and I know what tomorrow will bring.

Bariloche has changed since my brother, Carlos, and I tramped up and down the hillsides, picking *calafate* berries. Legend says that once you have eaten *calafate*, you will always return to Patagonia. In my case, the legend holds true. But although Bariloche is still beautiful, boutiques and expensive homes and tourists from Brazil, North America, and Europe have changed the character of my rugged hometown. It feels more like a part of the modern world and less like a frontier village.

I have always wanted to go beyond the frontier, and whenever I do get there, I can hear silence. By that I mean I am very conscious of the Indians who once lived here. Mapuches, Tehuelches, Onas—there are still a few there in the most hidden parts of Patagonia, but I hear their spirit everywhere.

The Indians are the ones who first brought fire to this land. In my native region, I learned from the Mapuches, who still cook by burying their feasts, surrounded by hot rocks, a rustic style of communal cooking called *curanto*. They cooked whole llamas this way and Patagonian ostriches. The Incas, in the hot arid lands that border the Atacama Desert (where astronomers say the air is the clearest of any place on earth), built double-decker fires, separated by flat stones. That technique became the basis for my *infiernillo*. From the Charrúas Indians of the semitropical area we call the Littoral,

I learned to cook on wooden stakes at the side of a campfire.

When the Indians left, pushed out by the Europeans, the gauchos, our cowboys, with their blousy pants and fearsome daggers that left knife scars as a testament of manhood, perfected the *parrilla:* cooking on grates over live coals. I have spent many nights camping in the wild with my makeshift *parrilla.* Finally, the bricklayers and carpenters and dockworkers of Buenos Aires taught me the simplest method of all: cooking on a *chapa.* For them, it was often simply a piece of sheet metal thrown over a fire. The makeshift griddle heated up quickly, so they could cook their sausages and churrasco steaks during the precious minutes of their lunch hour. You will see my version of *chapa* cooking throughout this book.

It was from the traditions of those Indians and cowboys, carpenters, and stevedores that I learned to take all that I had learned in the temples of European gastronomy as a young chef and simplify and adapt it to cooking with fire. The knowledge I gained in France and Italy about building flavor and working with the best ingredients, about sautéing, and about baking stood me in good stead as I traveled around Argentina experimenting with fire. I have always felt the lure of travel, absorbing influences wherever I go. In time, I began to bring my fires with me.

I went to bustling New York and elegant Paris, to the ineffably beautiful coast of Northern California, to my own farm in the green hills of Uruguay, and to the wild coast of Patagonia in the province of Chubut, where improbably graceful right whales still come to mate each year, and where sea lions congregate on the shore, giving lusty voice to their basso chorus.

And as I traveled, I left myself open to the seasons and the memories and the ingredients that were as surely a part of my baggage as my shirts and blue jeans. When you travel, you cook with what is there, not with what you want to be there. That forces you to think and create. In the course of my travels

for this book, I began to experiment more and more. I fell in love with the idea of charring and burning the herbs and greens that I use for salads, marinades, and dressings (see page 122). In Peter Kaminsky's backyard in Cobble Hill, Brooklyn, I took the idea of the Argentine *asado*—a beef extravaganza—and created a "parade of pork" (see page 116). A trip to Northern California introduced me to the caramel-sweet delicata squash (see page 112). Some herb oils left overnight in the fridge suggested the array of chilled flavored oils that now replace herb butter on many of my grilled dishes (see page 281).

Throughout my travels, I found myself encountering new challenges and new ideas that became new recipes.

A passionate encounter between wanderlust and cooking is what this book is all about. But then, that is what my life has always been about—love, wandering the world, and making food. It is who I am. Maybe someday I will build a restaurant on the Brooklyn waterfront, or on wild Bolinas Bay, or in some Parisian back alley. I still feel as if my travels have only just begun, and wherever I go, I will take the fires of Patagonia with me.

I have always wanted to
go beyond the frontier,
and whenever I get
there, I can hear silence.

MY FIRES

Many of the recipes in this book were prepared
on a portable grill that accompanies me on
my travels. Just like you might pack a favorite
sweater for a journey, I take my grill, baptized in
Patagonian fire, wherever I go. For this book I
traveled from Patagonia to Paris, from Buenos
Aires to Brooklyn, from Brazil to Berkeley
locating new ingredients, building fires, making
meals that let fire work its timeless magic. All
I need—all anyone needs—for this primal
pleasure is flame and food, and the hunger
that inspires the chef in all of us. It doesn't
matter how elaborate or simple the cooking
setup is. If there is wood or charcoal to burn,
and local ingredients to be had, one can find a
way to make something delicious.

Parrilla (Grill)

When North Americans think of grilling, this is the method they have in mind. We Argentines are very partial to the *parrilla,* especially for meats, fish, and poultry. A *parrilla* is nothing more than a grate set over hot coals. You can achieve a similar effect indoors with a ridged grill pan, although you will never get the woodsy aroma that is the signature of food cooked over fire. If you do grill indoors, a well-ventilated cooking area is a must.

If you have the room for it, I suggest a cast-iron grate about 36 by 30 inches set about 9 inches above the ground. I like the generosity of space that a large cooking surface offers; whether you crust, char, or simply heat, you want space around the ingredients so that they cook uniformly and don't steam or stew. Cinder blocks will serve quite well to give your fire the right elevation. Bricks work too. Don't be afraid of improvising with what you have on hand. The important thing is to have enough space for your fire and your food. It doesn't matter if the setup doesn't look fancy—the food won't know the difference.

Chapa (Griddle)

A traditional *chapa* is simply a big, flat piece of tin set over a fire. Its chief virtue is that once you've built your fire under it, instead of waiting for your coals to burn down to an ideal cooking temperature, you are ready to cook in minutes, as soon as the *chapa* is hot. I prefer a *chapa* made of cast iron. *Plancha* is the word in Spain for this type of cooking surface, and I use the terms interchangeably.

For more ambitious *chapa* cooking, if there is someone in your area who makes cast-iron doors, gates, or fences, you could have him make you a *chapa* big enough for a family cookout. I suggest one 30 by 30 inches set about 12 to 15 inches off the ground. Of course, not everyone has the luxury of space for a *chapa*; a cast-iron skillet or grill will also do the trick. After you've cooked with a *chapa* for a while, you will learn to "read" the heat of your cast-iron cooking surface. If it develops a white patina, you have really high heat; a uniformly black surface is less hot.

One of the virtues of cast iron is its ability to maintain even heat, because of both its thickness and the dense nature of iron. Whether you are cooking indoors or out with cast iron, give it 5 to 10 minutes of preheating in order to heat all the way through.

Rescoldo (Embers and Ashes)

I originally learned about cooking in embers from Argentine gauchos, who would place some eggs, potatoes, squash, and other vegetables in the embers of their breakfast fires before they went to tend their cattle in the morning. When they returned, the food was cooked. It is so elemental and so simple. I have begun to do fruit this way. *Rescoldo* oranges are a new favorite and among the most delicious things you can imagine.

People often ask me about the taste of the ashes. If you dust things off well, and if you then peel the skins of whatever vegetables you have cooked, there are no ashes to speak of—although, truthfully, I like the taste of a little ash.

While the gauchos and Indians cooked their *rescoldo* food in the embers of outdoor fires, a home fireplace works just as well.

Horno (Brick or Clay Oven)

An *horno de barro* is our version of a wood-burning oven of the kind that more and more North American restaurants are using for pizzas, breads, and roasted meat and fish. Many home cooks have built these ovens in their own backyards. It is a marvelous way to cook: great uniform heat and wood-smoke flavor! All ovens are a little different and all types of wood burn differently, so cooking this way requires a period of practice.

I sometimes call for adjusting the heat during the cooking process. If using a wood-fired oven, you can move the coals and wood around and place the food nearer or farther from the heat to raise or lower the temperature. You can gauge the heat with an infrared oven thermometer. For those of you without a wood-burning oven, I give temperatures and timings for a conventional oven.

Iron: Ancient, Wonderful, Practical

My grill is made of cast iron, as are my *chapa* and my skillets. There is something comforting about cooking with this ancient material. Our ancestors used it for thousands of years before the advent of steel and aluminum. It is the original nonstick surface (although occasionally I prefer things to stick and tear away; I find the texture more interesting). In my home and restaurant kitchens, copper also has its place, but for the brutal heat and extreme conditions of outdoor cooking, iron is my constant partner.

A grill with heavy cast-iron grates—¼ to ½ inch thick—results in two different types of heat. On the one hand, the food is exposed to radiant heat from the spaces between the iron bars, and on the other, the iron itself heats up to transfer heat evenly and directly to whatever you are cooking.

Although it is nothing more than a flat metal surface, a cast-iron *chapa* can be a sophisticated cooking tool. Depending on where you pile your coals under different parts of the *chapa,* you can have warm, hot, and superhot cooking areas simultaneously, which allows you to cook a number of different ingredients at the optimum heat levels: for example, onions over lower heat so that they slowly caramelize; eggs over a medium flame so that they cook through without burning or drying out; a skirt steak over a hotter spot so that it quickly develops a crust without overcooking the interior; and pears over medium-low heat so that their sugars caramelize and intensify the flavor.

To get the best sear or char, always preheat a cast-iron *chapa* or griddle for 5 to 10 minutes. Cast iron is dense and takes a while to heat up, but once it is hot, it holds the heat and conducts it evenly.

As for cleaning up, I find that cast iron is remarkably easy. I simply set the *chapa* over a very hot fire, then douse it with water and scrape it with a wire brush or a big spatula (a wide putty knife from the hardware store is perfect for this). Indoors, wipe out any fat with a rag or paper towels and rinse with hot water. If there is burnt-on food residue, use a stiff brush and coarse salt as an abrasive. Dry the pan immediately and give the surface a quick wipe with a lightly oiled paper towel. Never put cast iron in the dishwasher.

Hardwood Lump Charcoal— No Substitutes

For most of the recipes in this book, I grilled over charcoal because that was the most convenient way with my traveling grill, rather than starting with raw wood. I always use hardwood lump charcoal, not those nasty briquettes made of pressed sawdust. Lump charcoal burns like real wood, because it is real chunks of wood that have burned down a bit.

Chimney charcoal starters require only a few pieces of newspaper stuffed in the bottom and a match. No chemicals or other charcoal lighting products. I love them.

HOW HOT IS IT?

If you hold your hand about 4 inches from the cooking surface, you will quickly get a sense of how hot a fire is. Hold your hand above the cooking surface and start counting. If after 2 full seconds it is too hot to keep your hand there, that is high heat. Use the same technique to gauge the heat from any fire, with the timing in the chart below as a guideline.

2 seconds	**High heat**
3–4 seconds	**Medium-high heat**
5–6 seconds	**Medium heat**
7–8 seconds	**Medium-low heat**
8–12 seconds	**Low heat**

Don't rush your count: you want full seconds. We Argentines count *"Un matador, dos matadores,"* etc. Those whose native language is English go with "One Mississippi, two Mississippi."

Remember that when you are cooking out of doors, the weather can affect temperature and timing. Wind can blow heat away from the coals or can cause the coals to burn more intensely. Ambient air temperature also comes into play. Things often take longer to cook on cold days.

FEEDING THE FIRE

Think of fire as a love affair of a kind between heat and food. Like real love, it must be nurtured and replenished or the fire will go out and, with it, the passion that inspires our cooking.

One of the main differences between Argentine and North American styles of grilling is that we often add mature coals to the fire for longer cooking, rather than lighting more coals and waiting for them to burn down. The best way to do this is to start some more charcoal in a separate spot (a second grill or any fireproof surface is quite handy for this purpose). Then add the already burning coals to your cooking fire once they are uniformly glowing. Rake the coals into larger piles for high heat, or spread them out evenly for more even lower heat.

If you cook on a kettle-style grill, a hinged grate that lifts on both sides makes it easy to add more coals. But if your grill doesn't come equipped with a hinged grate, you can simply put on a pair of heavy-duty oven mitts, carefully lift the grate, set it to one side (away from dogs or cats!), and add mature coals to those already in the grill.

HOW MUCH CHARCOAL DO I NEED?
Five pounds of charcoal is certainly enough for a quick steak or some vegetables on the *chapa*. For anything that requires more time, have more charcoal on hand and ready to go. A three-hour leg of lamb with all the fixings could use up a 20-pound bag. If you do a lot of grilling, keep two 20-pound bags on hand so you won't get caught short. At some point, you are going to use them up.

How Long Should It Cook?

Meat varies from animal to animal and cut to cut. A large cut from a lean animal will have less fat in the muscle fibers, so the only way to avoid dry, tough meat is to serve it rare. Wild game, which feeds on grasses, nuts, and berries, gets a lot of exercise and quite often is lean, so it, too, is usually best served rare. But even with free-range animals, like pigs, lamb, and cattle, there are more marbled cuts, like the shoulder. These are suitable for longer cooking, allowing the collagen in the muscle fibers to melt, making the meat tender and juicy.

Vegetables, just like meat, have their own "preferences." Greens need a quick charring on a very hot *chapa*, while root vegetables need to cook slowly. My directive is: "Make the fire fit the food."

Take Your Time

There is so much you can do with a fire that you replenish for long cooking. At first, a charcoal fire burns hot, which is superb for grilling thin cuts of meat and vegetables on a *chapa*. Then, when the coals are covered with white ash, what I refer to as a mature bed of coals, the fire is suitable for caramelizing, slow-roasting—any *parrilla* recipe.

Almost any food can be made delicious when cooked over fire; each food has a particular stage of fire at which it cooks best. Listen to your ingredients—they will be your best guide—and keep your fire going all through the meal, including dessert. I know that busy people often don't have time for a two-hour grilling extravaganza, but when you do, I promise these will be the meals that are burnt into memory.

Be Safe

The first rule of cooking with fire is: be safe. Keep your precious self safe and keep our precious forests safe. An out-of-control fire is dangerous, especially on a windy day, far from the nearest fire department. So have an exit plan.

The best strategy is to build your fire near water. If hoses are practical, hook them up, test them, and have them ready. Full buckets of water, sand, or fine dry soil can also be used to dampen a fire. First, clear away any dry grass and tinder from the cooking area. Four or five feet of cleared ground is the minimum.

As kids in Patagonia, my brother and I often helped the volunteer fire squads, and I can still remember how one mighty gust of wind ignited half a mile of forest in thirty seconds! When you are trying to start a fire, or even light a match, wind is not your friend. But once a fire is blazing, wind can be a real hazard. You may start your outing on a perfect calm sunny day. By noon, especially in Patagonia, the morning zephyr may have become a Force 7 gale and your luncheon campfire may send embers flying in all directions, where they can easily ignite parched grass and dry timber. If you find yourself in this situation, move your grill grates and *chapa* aside if you can. Next, heave bucketfuls of sand or earth on the fire, followed by water. Your first priority is to contain the fire so that it doesn't spread. And remember, before you even think about saving your food, save the forest. You can always buy more food, but a forest takes a hundred years to grow back.

APPETIZERS AND SALADS

Charred Mushrooms
with Thyme and Garlic Toast

Fire loves mushrooms, and mushrooms love fire. When I cook them over hot coals, they bubble and then, just like meat, develop a beautiful crust. When I think of the combination of mushrooms and fire, I see an image of a blackened patch of forest on a Patagonian hillside outside of my hometown, Bariloche. It is some months after a wildfire, and shoots of green have just begun to sprout in the blackened earth. Because it rained the day before, all kinds of mushrooms have sprung up in the sunlight.

Mushrooms are high in umami, which is concentrated as they cook. The result is a flavor that can both stand up to the garlic and gain subtlety from the aroma of fresh thyme. Most mushrooms can be left whole. If they are in large clusters, like oyster mushrooms, cut them into manageable pieces (2 to 3 inches). **SERVES 4**

4 thick slices sourdough bread
1 garlic clove, cut in half
6 tablespoons extra virgin olive oil
2 teaspoons fresh thyme leaves
4 tablespoons unsalted butter
2 pounds assorted mushrooms, such as
    chanterelles, oyster, king oyster, and/or
    shiitakes, cleaned and trimmed (discard stems
    if using shiitakes)
2 lemons, halved
Coarse salt and freshly ground black pepper

Heat a *chapa* or a large cast-iron grill pan over medium heat. Grill the bread on both sides for a minute or two, pressing down slightly to mark it. Transfer it to a platter and rub one side of each slice with the cut garlic clove. Drizzle with about half the olive oil and sprinkle with half the thyme. Spread a tablespoon of butter on each slice of bread to melt into it.

Brush the mushrooms with the remaining oil and arrange in a single uncrowded layer on the *chapa* or grill pan. Cook on the first side until nicely marked, about 5 minutes. Turn and repeat until all sides are browned and the mushrooms are tender when pierced with a paring knife.

Meanwhile, grill the lemon halves, cut side down, until lightly browned.

Arrange the mushrooms on the slices of bread, sprinkle the remaining thyme over them, and season with salt and pepper. Serve immediately, with the grilled lemon halves on the side.

PRECEDING: Blistered Peppers with Charred Onions and Lemon Zest (page 45) on a *chapa*.

Grilled Carrots with Aged Ricotta and Oregano on Toast

This is one of those dishes where you think you know how it's going to taste before you try it, but then the combined flavors and textures are a delicious surprise. You may regard carrots as an everyday vegetable, not the kind of thing you serve for a special meal. This recipe settles the issue in favor of the carrot. Treat every ingredient with respect, and it will reward you. **SERVES 4**

4 carrots, peeled

1 red onion

About ½ cup extra virgin olive oil, plus more for drizzling

¼ cup fresh oregano leaves

Coarse salt and freshly ground black pepper

8 ounces aged ricotta or ricotta salata, cut into ¼-inch-thick slices

4 large garlic cloves (or 2 elephant garlic cloves), thinly sliced

4 large slices sourdough bread

Grated zest of 1 large lemon

Trim the carrots and slice lengthwise ⅛ inch thick on a mandoline. Slice the onion paper-thin on the mandoline. Pour ¼ cup of the olive oil onto a wide rimmed plate and sprinkle with the oregano and salt and pepper to taste. This will be your dressing for the carrots and ricotta.

Heat a charcoal grill or a large ridged cast-iron grill pan over very high heat. Brush the grill or pan with oil. When it starts to smoke, arrange the carrot slices across the grill ridges and grill for 2 to 3 minutes, or until they are nicely striped on the bottom. Turn and repeat on the other side, then transfer to the plate of dressing and turn to coat.

Brush the grill with oil again and add the ricotta. Grill until nicely marked on the first side, then turn and repeat. Add to the dressing and turn to coat them too.

Combine the garlic and onion with 2 tablespoons of the olive oil in a small bowl.

Heat a *chapa* or a cast-iron griddle over medium heat and brush with olive oil. Scatter the sliced garlic and onion over the bread slices and press down firmly on them with a spatula to make them adhere as much as possible. Invert the bread onto the hot griddle and cook for about 2 minutes, until the bread is toasted and the garlic and onions are lightly browned. Using a wide spatula, carefully scrape up the bread, with the garlic and onions, from the griddle and flip over onto a platter; retrieve any loose garlic and onions and scatter over the bread. Add the grilled carrots and ricotta to the toasts, and sprinkle the grated lemon zest over the top. Season with salt and pepper to taste, drizzle with olive oil, and serve.

Red and Golden Beet Salad with Radishes and Soft-Boiled Eggs

This is one of the few fresh vegetable salads you can put together all through the winter. It is a favorite at my restaurant in Garzón, even in the summer. Very crunchy, very fresh. The eggs make it a complete light meal. I first had it on a trip to Australia with a number of other chefs, including David Tanis. If you don't know David, he has had a very interesting life: For many years, he spent half the year as the chef at Chez Panisse and the other half of the year as a private chef in Paris. Now his recipes appear every week in *The New York Times* Dining section, and they are a highlight of my Wednesday morning reading.

SERVES 4

1½ tablespoons fresh thyme leaves
2 tablespoons fresh lemon juice
**6 tablespoons extra virgin olive oil, plus more for
    drizzling**
Coarse salt and freshly ground black pepper
2 golden beets
2 red beets
2 carrots
2 large radishes
4 large eggs

Pound 1 tablespoon of the thyme leaves in a mortar until they are bruised and start to form a paste. Whisk in 1½ tablespoons of the lemon juice, and then the olive oil. Season to taste with salt and pepper. Set aside.

Peel and grate first the golden and then the red beets on the coarse blade of a box grater, keeping the colors separate. Toss the golden beets with the remaining 1½ teaspoons lemon juice. Grate the carrots and reserve. Thinly slice the radishes on a mandoline and reserve.

Cook the eggs in a saucepan of boiling water for 4 minutes if at sea level, a minute longer if at higher altitude. Run under cold water to cool slightly, then carefully peel off the shells.

Arrange the grated beets, carrots, and radish slices attractively on a wide platter. Gently tear the soft eggs open and arrange in the center of the platter. Season with salt, pepper, and the remaining 1½ teaspoons thyme leaves. Drizzle with the vinaigrette and serve.

Beet and Orange Salad with Arugula and Feta (page 30).

Beet and Orange Salad with Arugula and Feta

Sweet beets, sharp red onion, and slightly tangy, sweet orange all make strong flavor statements that stand out like soloists in a jazz combo. The salty, creamy feta pulls them together into a harmonic whole. When I can find them, I use navel oranges from Corrientes and Entre Rios, in our tropical north. We call them *umbilicus,* which sounds quite sexy to me. **SERVES 4**

1 large red beet
1 large golden beet
1 navel orange
1 red onion
2 cups baby arugula
2 ounces feta cheese
2 teaspoons fresh thyme leaves
Coarse sea salt and freshly ground black pepper
Extra virgin olive oil for drizzling

Heat an *horno* or the oven to 375°F.

Wrap each beet in foil and roast for 1 hour, or until they are tender all the way through when pierced with a skewer.

While the beets are roasting, using a sharp knife, slice off the peel from the orange, carefully removing all the pith. Slice thinly.

Slice the onion very thin on a mandoline.

When the beets are done, let them cool enough to handle, then remove the skin and slice them about ⅓ inch thick, keeping the colors separate so they don't bleed into each other.

Arrange most of the arugula, the beet slices, sliced onion, and orange segments on a wide platter. Crumble the feta over the top and add the rest of the arugula and the thyme. Season with salt, pepper, and a good drizzle of olive oil and serve.

PICTURED ON PAGES 28–29

Fig Salad with Burrata and Basil

I first discovered burrata when I was working in a wonderful restaurant, San Domenico, in the town of Imola in Emilia-Romagna, Italy. Burrata has three distinct textures: a soft skin; an interior layer of smooth, solid mozzarella; and a core of beautiful cream. It needs crunchy sea salt for both texture and flavor. Tearing the figs by hand is very important to the look of this dish—it is seductively rustic. **SERVES 4**

4 large fresh figs
1 burrata, about 7 ounces
12 large fresh basil leaves, torn
Coarse sea salt and freshly ground black pepper
1 lemon, halved
Extra virgin olive oil for drizzling

Tear the figs open and arrange them in a wide shallow bowl.

Pat the burrata dry, tear it into 4 large pieces, and nestle them among the torn figs. Tear the basil leaves into pieces and scatter over the figs and cheese.

Season to taste with salt, pepper, lemon juice, and a good drizzle of olive oil.

Tomato and Avocado Salad

This salad relies completely on the quality of its ingredients—ripe Hass avocados and heirloom tomatoes at their peak, perfect basil leaves, and seriously good olive oil. Then a squeeze of lemon, fleur de sel, and a few grinds of black pepper are all that's required. **SERVES 4**

2 ripe Hass avocados
1 lemon, halved
2½ pounds heirloom tomatoes, cut into cubes
12 large perfect fresh basil leaves, torn
Fleur de sel
Freshly ground black pepper
Extra virgin olive oil for drizzling

Halve the avocados, remove the pits, and coat the cut surfaces with lemon juice to prevent darkening. Arrange on individual plates with the tomatoes and basil. Season to taste with fleur de sel and pepper, and drizzle with olive oil.

Griddled Red Bartlett Pears Wrapped in Iberico Ham

This simple dish is cooked on a *chapa,* and the crispness of the ham and the softness of the pears provide a delicious contrast of textures. Made with only four ingredients, it is a dish I like not only for its flavor, but also because it can be ready for guests within a few minutes of starting a fire. Iberico ham has the nuance of flavor of the finest Burgundy from the vineyards of Romanée-Conti. In Spain, the ham is often served with a medium-dry sherry. Here, the fruitiness, acidity, and sweetness of the pear achieve the same result.

If you can't get Iberico, regular serrano ham or prosciutto or even country ham is a good choice. **SERVES 4**

4 ripe Red Bartlett or Anjou pears
12 thin slices Iberico ham
Coarse sea salt and freshly ground black pepper

Slice the (unpeeled) pears about ½ inch thick (see photo, page 34). You should get 3 good slices out of each pear.

Heat a *chapa* or a large cast-iron griddle over low heat. Wrap each slice of pear in a slice of ham and arrange them seam side down on the hot surface. Cook until the fruit begins to soften and the ham is crisp on the bottom, about 3 minutes. Turn carefully, sprinkle with salt and pepper, and continue cooking until the pears are tender and the ham on the second side is crisp, about 3 minutes more. Serve immediately.

PICTURED ON PAGE 35

Griddled Red Bartlett Pears Wrapped in Iberico Ham (page 33).

Griddled Cheeses with Parsley, Red Onion, and Cherry Tomatoes

When I have friends over for an *asado,* I follow the traditional Argentine routine of serving a few *picadas* (small bites) before moving on to the carnivore's cornucopia. Melted cheeses are usually the first thing that you can offer straight from the *chapa,* within minutes of lighting the fire. Different cheeses will melt in different ways, and they will crust up differently as well. Some are chewy, some softer, some more burnt or browned. You will know when they look melty enough—it's not an exact science. **SERVES 4**

Extra virgin olive oil

8 ounces good grilling or melting cheese, such as haloumi, kasseri, Comté, or provolone, sliced into wedges or slices about 1 inch thick

1 small red onion, very thinly sliced

½ pint each red and orange cherry tomatoes, halved

1 cup fresh flat-leaf parsley leaves

Sea salt and freshly ground black pepper

Grilled bread

Heat a *chapa* or a large cast-iron griddle over low heat until a drop of water sizzles on the surface. Brush it with olive oil and place the cheese wedges or slices on the griddle, spaced well apart. Cook for about 2 minutes, without moving them, until the bottom is nicely browned and the cheese is beginning to soften or melt. Use a sharp spatula or scraper to transfer the cheese, browned side up, to a serving platter. If you are using a soft cheese, gently but firmly squeeze the pieces into an attractive scrunched shape.

Arrange the onion and tomatoes on the platter, scatter the parsley over the top, and drizzle with olive oil. Season with salt and a few grinds of pepper. Serve with grilled bread.

OPPOSITE: Four different cheeses, melting on a *chapa.*
Clockwise from top left: provolone, kasseri, Comté, and haloumi.

Shaved Artichokes a la Plancha with Aged Comté Cheese

The beauty of this dish is that you get some of the crispiness (but much less of the fat) of the famous deep-fried artichokes of the Roman Jewish ghetto, *carciofi alia giudia,* along with the softness of steamed artichokes. I know that cleaning artichokes is not a favorite kitchen task, but the result is worth it. I still remember my very first day as an apprentice in the kitchens of Ledoyen in Paris. No sooner had I arrived than I was sent to trim eight cases of artichokes, about four hundred of them. So when people complain that a few artichokes are too difficult or time-consuming to prep, I advise them to keep it in perspective.

Comté cheese has a hint of the nuttiness of artichokes. If Comté is unavailable, Gruyère works well. SERVES 4

3 lemons

4 large artichokes

¼ cup extra virgin olive oil, plus extra for the *chapa*

Coarse salt and freshly ground black pepper

4 ounces aged Comté or Gruyère cheese,
   coarsely grated

Grilled bread

Cut one of the lemons in half, squeeze the juice into a large bowl of cold water, and toss in the squeezed-out rind as well. As you trim the artichokes, remember to dip the newly exposed areas into this acidulated water to prevent them from turning brown.

Pick up an artichoke and snap off all the tough outer leaves. Cut off the end of the stem. Lay the artichoke on its side on a cutting board and, with a sharp serrated knife, slice off the rest of the leaves at the point where they meet the wide base. With a small sharp knife, peel off the dark green fibrous layer around the base and the stem. Cut the artichoke lengthwise in half and scoop out the fuzzy choke with a sharp spoon. Immerse in the acidulated water. Repeat with the rest of the artichokes.

Squeeze the juice from the remaining 2 lemons into a bowl. Whisk in ¼ cup of the olive oil to blend.

With a watchful eye on your fingers, slice the artichoke hearts paper-thin on a mandoline, tossing them immediately into the oil and lemon juice mixture to coat.

Heat a *chapa* or a large cast-iron griddle over medium heat and brush generously with oil. When the oil shimmers, spread the artichokes out on the hot surface and drizzle with a little more oil. They will start to crisp and brown after a minute or two. Don't let them get too dark—you want them to be a nutty golden color to retain some softness. Turn with a wide spatula to lightly brown the other side. As the bottom side cooks, season the top with salt and pepper and scatter the grated cheese evenly over it. When the cheese has melted, scoop the artichokes and cheese together with two wide spatulas, then transfer to a serving dish and serve immediately with grilled bread.

A long and lazy midsummer lunch in Trancoso, Brazil (see pages 234–239).

Chicken Livers a la Plancha in Charred Endive

Creamy, crusty, deeply meaty in flavor, chicken livers are too often overlooked. Here they are the star. You want to use good ones, though, from a top-quality chicken. They need lots of space between them on the hot *chapa* so they get very crunchy but are still quite pink inside. Char just the edges of the endive leaves. Put a piece of liver on a burnt endive leaf, and you're ready to eat. **SERVES 4**

8 ounces fresh chicken livers
¼ cup parsley oil (see page 281), at room temperature
Coarse salt and freshly ground black pepper
1 heaping tablespoon Dijon mustard
12 large perfect endive leaves

Wash the livers and carefully trim off any fat or gristle. Separate or cut the lobes into 12 bite-sized pieces and pat them thoroughly dry on paper towels. Spread 2 tablespoons of the parsley oil on a plate, add the livers, and turn them to coat well. Season well with salt and pepper.

Whisk the mustard and the remaining 2 tablespoons parsley oil in a medium bowl. Season with salt and pepper, then lightly toss the endive leaves in the mixture to coat. Transfer the leaves to a plate, rounded side up.

Heat a *chapa* or two large cast-iron griddles over high heat until a drop of water sizzles on the surface. Using tongs, place the endive leaves rounded side up on the hot surface and cook, without moving them, for 2 minutes, or until the edges are well charred. Remove them with tongs and arrange rounded side down on a serving platter.

Arrange the livers at least an inch apart on a clean part of the *chapa* or in one of the griddles, and cook, without moving them, for 2 minutes, or until you see from the side that they are browned and crisp on the bottom. (Do this in batches if necessary.) Turn them over and cook for a minute or two more, until they are crisp all over but still quite pink within. As the livers are done, place them on the endive leaves. Serve immediately.

A *chapa* placed in the hearth of my kitchen fireplace.

Ensalada de Sopa Paraguaya

The cornmeal-based bread known as *sopa Paraguaya* was born, so the story goes, of a mistake. Carlos Antonio López, the first (and the stoutest) president of Paraguay, liked a thick soup of cornmeal, cheese, and milk. One day, his chef made it too thick. Turning necessity into a virtue, he popped it into a bread pan and baked it. El Presidente loved it, and so have generations of Paraguayans ever since. I decided to use the savory and satisfying bread as the basis for a kind of panzanella, adding avocados and tomatoes. **SERVES 4**

1 tablespoon brown sugar

Juice of 2 lemons

½ cup oaky extra virgin olive oil, plus more for brushing

2 ripe avocados, halved, pitted, peeled, and diced

2 ripe tomatoes, diced

Coarse salt and freshly ground black pepper

½ cup fresh cilantro leaves, torn into pieces

½ recipe Sopa Paraguaya (page 266), torn into 1-inch chunks

4 slices Sun-Dried Tomatoes (page 285)

Heat a *chapa* or a large cast-iron griddle over medium heat.

Meanwhile, prepare the vinaigrette: Dissolve the brown sugar in the lemon juice in a small bowl. Gradually whisk in the olive oil until it is well emulsified.

Put the avocados and tomatoes in a large bowl and toss them together with half the vinaigrette. Season with salt and pepper. Add the cilantro and toss again.

Brush the *chapa* or griddle with olive oil, and when it shimmers, add the sopa chunks and sear for a minute or two, until they are nicely charred on the bottom. (Do this in batches if necessary to give them plenty of space.) If the cheese oozes onto the skillet, just scrape it up with a spatula. As the chunks are charred, transfer them to the salad bowl and toss gently. Check the seasoning and add more salt or pepper if necessary.

Divide the salad among four serving plates, heaping it into a pyramid on each one. Drizzle with more vinaigrette to taste and top with the sun-dried tomatoes. Serve immediately.

Crunchy Potato Skins with Parsley

I started making this recipe in my restaurants with the skins of oven-roasted potatoes left over after we'd used most of the insides for gnocchi. Think of them as big, rugged, free-form French fries that are cooked first in the oven. The hot oil is just for crisping. I first tasted vinegar on fried potatoes at Mary's Fish Camp in Greenwich Village. I later learned that in New England (and Old England), vinegar is often served with deep-fried food. It refreshes the palate after the hot oil and potato starch. These are great served with drinks. **SERVES 4**

4 Idaho (baking) potatoes, scrubbed
A small bunch of flat-leaf parsley,
   tough stems removed
8 cups olive oil for deep frying, preferably extra
   virgin
Coarse salt
Red wine vinegar for drizzling

Heat an *horno* or the oven to 375°F.

Prick the potatoes with a fork and put them on the center oven rack. Bake for 50 minutes to an hour, until they are tender all the way through when pierced with a skewer. Remove from the oven and allow them to cool enough for you to handle.

Cut the potatoes in half, then scoop out most of the flesh and reserve for another use. Tear the skins into large, rough pieces. Let them dry out on a tray lined with paper towels for at least 15 minutes.

Line another tray with paper towels for draining the potatoes when they come out of the oil. Tear the parsley into rough pieces and set aside.

Heat the oil in a deep pot to 360°F, or until a small piece of potato bubbles when dropped in the pot. Fry the potatoes, in batches if necessary, until golden brown and crunchy, 1 to 2 minutes. Remove the potatoes with a skimmer and transfer to the paper towels to drain. Season to taste with salt, scatter with the parsley, and serve with vinegar on the side. (Reserve strained oil for reuse, and refrigerate.)

Blistered Peppers with Charred Onions and Lemon Zest

Step up to any tapas bar in Spain and you are pretty sure to find a plate of *pimientos de Padrón*—blistered small peppers from Galicia, fried in olive oil and salted. They are kind of the Russian roulette of the pepper world in that while they are usually mild, about one in ten is quite hot. The lemon zest adds some fresh, fruity acidity.

In the United States, we rarely see Padrón peppers; shishito peppers, available in Asian markets and some farmers' markets, work equally well, but they, too, are occasionally hot. **SERVES 8**

Extra virgin olive oil
1 pound small mild peppers (see headnote)
1 small onion, thinly sliced
½ cup fresh flat-leaf parsley leaves
Grated zest of 1 lemon
Fleur de sel
Freshly ground black pepper

Heat a *chapa* or a large cast-iron griddle over high heat. Brush it with oil, and when the oil shimmers, add the peppers and cook for about 4 minutes, until they become blistered and lightly charred on the bottom. Turn the peppers, brush the hot surface with a little more oil, and cook them on the other side for several minutes, until they are softened and browned.

Meanwhile, clear a small space on one side of the *chapa,* brush it with more oil, and add the onions and parsley. Scatter half the lemon zest over everything, season to taste with fleur de sel and pepper, and turn the onions and parsley to brown on the other side, adding more oil if necessary.

Transfer everything to a small platter as it is done, taking care not to burn the onions. Scatter with the remaining lemon zest and serve immediately.

PICTURED ON PAGE 20

Tuna Tartare with Crunchy Bread Crumbs

Uncomplicated, straightforward, and clean tasting: these are the qualities I strive for in a recipe. This one comes from Tomas Scarpetti, a terrific young Argentine chef who has cooked in a number of my restaurants. I am happy to report that whenever we offer it, we completely sell out. **SERVES 4**

4 large eggs
1 pound fresh yellowfin tuna steaks
Extra virgin olive oil for drizzling
1 cup Crunchy Bread Crumbs (page 290)
2 tablespoons fresh lemon juice
Freshly ground black pepper
1 small bunch chives, chopped
Fleur de sel

Cook the eggs in a saucepan of boiling water for 4 minutes if at sea level, a minute longer if at higher altitude. Run under cold water and then carefully peel off the shells.

Slice the tuna ¼ inch thick. Stack the slices a few at a time and cut against the grain into ¼-inch-wide strips, then cut into ¼-inch cubes.

Drizzle a little olive oil onto each of four serving plates and scatter the bread crumbs over them. Mound a portion of tuna on each plate and sprinkle with the lemon juice. Season with pepper, sprinkle with the chives, and drizzle with olive oil. Gently break a soft-boiled egg open onto each plate and sprinkle the eggs with fleur de sel. Serve immediately.

Potato Salad
with Black Olives

You are probably familiar with German potato salad made by dousing cooked potatoes with vinaigrette while they are still warm, then tossing them with pungent onions just before serving to wake up the palate. Here, I add smashed olives and oregano, which contribute texture, saltiness, and a distinct herbal note.

Potatoes, just like me, are natives of South America. They were first grown in the high plateaus of the Andes, and I believe that the very best potatoes for salad come from there, because, at such high altitudes, they have to struggle to grow. This gives them a coarse structure that is well suited to absorbing dressing. **SERVES 4**

2 pounds small red potatoes, scrubbed
Coarse salt
1 tablespoon Dijon mustard
3 tablespoons red wine vinegar
¼ cup plus 3 tablespoons extra virgin olive oil
Freshly ground black pepper
1 red onion, finely chopped
¼ cup fresh oregano leaves, roughly torn
12 pitted black olives, smashed

Put the potatoes in a saucepan with salted water to cover by about 2 inches and bring to a boil over medium-high heat. Turn the heat down and simmer the potatoes gently for about 12 minutes, or until they are tender all the way through when pierced with a skewer. Do not overcook, or they will break up when sliced. Drain.

While the potatoes are cooking, make the vinaigrette: Whisk together the mustard and red wine vinegar in a bowl until well blended. Gradually whisk in the olive oil until emulsified. Season to taste with salt and pepper.

When the drained potatoes are still hot but cool enough to handle, pat them dry with paper towels and slice them about ⅓ inch thick. Put them in a large bowl, add the vinaigrette, and turn them gently in it, taking care not to break the slices. Check the seasoning and add more salt or pepper it necessary.

Arrange the potatoes on a wide platter. Scatter the onions over the top, then the oregano and olives. Serve at room temperature.

Shaved Hearts of Celery with Portobello Mushrooms and Meyer Lemon

The crunch of the celery plays off well here against the smoothness of the mushrooms. Meyer lemons have a sweeter, less acidic flavor than regular lemons. This is a surprisingly savory dish; in part this is because of the umami of mushrooms, and the Grana Padano is also high in this hard-to-describe but powerful taste. I prefer cheese here to the anchovies that Romans use in their version of this recipe.

Serve with slices of country bread and a good Pinot Noir. Why not white wine, you ask? While a white is the traditional way to go with salads, pinot noir is also quite light. I love playing against type, and I enjoy the contrast of a red wine with a salad.

SERVES 4

1 large celery heart, leaves removed and reserved
1 large portobello mushroom cap, wiped clean
1 lemon, preferably a Meyer lemon
A chunk of Grana Padano for shaving (you want
  1½ ounces shaved cheese)
Extra virgin olive oil for drizzling
Sea salt and freshly ground black pepper

Slice the celery heart very thin on a mandoline and place in a bowl. Tear the leaves into bite-size pieces. Reserve separately.

Slice the mushroom cap very thin on the mandoline. Add to the bowl with the sliced celery.

Cut the lemon in half. Squeeze the juice of one half over the mushrooms and celery and toss very lightly. Cut the other half in half again.

Arrange the sliced mushrooms and celery on a platter and scatter the reserved leaves around them. Shave the Grana Padano over the top. Drizzle with olive oil, season with salt and pepper, and garnish with the reserved lemon wedges.

PICTURED ON PAGE 51

OPPOSITE: In table settings, as in recipes, contrast always makes things more notable.
ABOVE: Shaved Hearts of Celery with Portobello Mushrooms and Meyer Lemon (page 49).

Endive Salad with Mustard, Aged Goat Cheese, and Toasted Walnuts

Back when I had my first restaurant, I read a lot about French food. I somehow thought I could just show up in Paris one day, say, "Here I am," and get a job. Not surprisingly, I received zero offers. Still, on my first trip there, I got to eat lovely food. I can still recall the endive and Roquefort salad that woke up my palate. However, when I came back, Bariloche, the only Roquefort I could find, was mediocre.

Many years later, in Paris for my TV show, I went to Barthélémy, a famous cheese shop, where I saw not Roquefort, but delicious buttons of Crottin de Chavignol, an aged goat cheese.

I serve this on a wide platter, not piled in a salad bowl. That way, you can pick and choose which taste or texture you want next. **SERVES 4**

3 tablespoons spicy Dijon mustard
1 tablespoon red wine vinegar
½ cup extra virgin olive oil
Coarse salt and freshly ground black pepper
1 cup chopped fresh flat-leaf parsley
4 large endives, leaves separated
1 button aged Crottin de Chavignol
    (or 2 to 3 ounces other aged goat cheese)
½ cup toasted walnuts (see page 283)
½ cup Crunchy Bread Crumbs (page 290)

Whisk together the mustard and vinegar in a medium bowl. Whisk in the olive oil in a slow, steady stream until emulsified. Season with salt and pepper. Stir in the parsley.

Toss the endive in the vinaigrette and arrange on a wide serving platter. Crumble the cheese over the endives, then sprinkle the walnuts and bread crumbs over the salad. Serve immediately.

Pear Salad with Mint, Blue Cheese, and Fresh Dates

The dates for my first try at this recipe came from a farm in Southern California that supplies Alice Waters and a few lucky chefs. Those dates are so much in demand that the small production is allocated like the finest rare Bordeaux. But if you are not a superfamous chef, I wouldn't worry about it too much—chances are the dates in your market will be wonderful in this salad, alongside a full-flavored blue cheese and a touch of mint. You must serve it with slices of buttered bread—no French cheese lover would leave butter off the table, as I learned from my first mentor in France, Francis Trocellier, chef of Ledoyen in Paris. Every day he would have a wedge of cheese placed before him, along with a piece of bread and some butter, which he would slather on quite liberally; he'd have a salad alongside. This is my homage to him. **SERVES 4**

2 ripe Red Bartlett pears
8 ounces excellent American blue cheese,
    such as Rogue Creamery blue,
    cut into 4 wedges
12 soft fresh dates, such as Medjool
¼ cup fresh mint leaves
Sea salt and freshly ground black pepper
Extra virgin olive oil for drizzling
Good country bread and butter

Cut the pears in half, remove the stems and cores, and slice into wedges about ⅓ inch thick.

Divide the pears among four salad plates. Arrange a wedge of cheese and 3 dates on each plate and scatter the mint leaves over them. Season the pears lightly with salt and pepper and drizzle with olive oil. Serve with sliced country bread and butter on the side.

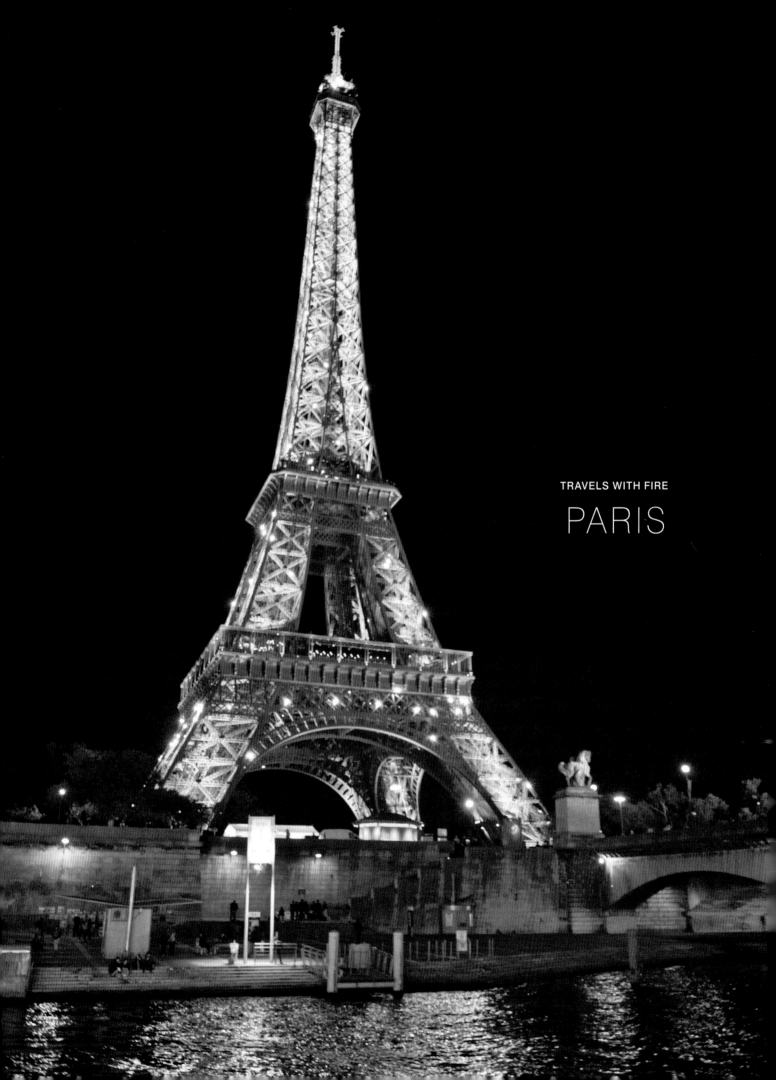

TRAVELS WITH FIRE

PARIS

"If you are lucky enough to have lived in Paris as a young man, then wherever you go for the rest of your life, it stays with you, for Paris is a moveable feast." Like much that Hemingway wrote, those words have stayed with me since I read them many years ago.

When I first went to France, I was, as were many chefs my age, enthralled with the revolution presided over by young chefs such as Alain Chapel, Alain Senderens, and Roger Vergé. From the vantage point of the passing years, it is remarkable to me that what has remained in my heart is not their nouvelle cuisine, but the tastes of the classic dishes at Ledoyen, Taillevent, and Le Grand Véfour, three of the bastions of traditional French cuisine. The rich and deeply flavored *ris de veau;* poached chicken with truffles under the skin; crispy, airy *pommes soufflées*: these are the languages of flavor I learned in France and still try to express with my fires. To me, this type of cooking is deep, elemental, and satisfying.

I also loved the division of labor in French kitchens: the *chef de partie*, the *poissonier*, the *rôtisseur*, the *entremetier*, the *saucier*, the *garde manger*, and the *patissier*. It is meticulous, careful, and very measured, a far cry from the crash and bang and hurry of many modern restaurants, even at the highest level. Although I don't preside over such a regimented kitchen, the notion that things take time and must be attended to with a watchful eye is at the heart of my cooking.

So when I took my Patagonian fires on the road, I very much wanted to return to France, and especially Paris. I love walking there, and the way the river divides the city, with a laid-back young people's half on the Left Bank and the more serious haute bourgeois life of the Right Bank. And then the

people! Their idiosyncrasies endear them to me. The way they eat, and drink, and dress . . . all seem so right. A croissant in the morning or a boiled egg in the shell. Steak frites for lunch or herring and potatoes.

And, of course, I adore the way everybody has lovers. The French don't talk about it much: it is too serious and too beautiful.

As I think about France and the years when I worked at restaurants in and out of Paris, it always calls to mind my experience with Alain Chapel. He was a genius and at first wanted nothing to do with me. I was quite young and had just started cooking professionally. I bought myself a Michelin Guide and wrote to all twenty-one three-star restaurants, offering to come work in their kitchens for free. Some responded with invitations, and so each year I would go work in one for a few months. Chapel was

never interested. But I persisted. I ambushed him in his garden one day, and he finally made me an offer. I could sign a contract and work for four years as a paid employee, or I could come for ten days and pay $1,000 per day.

At the time, I had a job in an elegant Buenos Aires restaurant and the owner said he would pay my way, so I went for ten days. Chapel was quite rough on me in the kitchen.

Then, on the last day, I was allowed to eat lunch in the dining room. Chapel joined me for half an hour.

"I know I have been tough, but I was testing you. I can see you really like cooking and that you can be very good at it."

I was so happy at that moment! The next day, I went to settle up and pay my tuition. I asked for the bill. Monsieur Chapel said, "What bill? There is no bill."

LIGHT MEALS

Huevos Escrachados with Pancetta, Zucchini Ribbons, and Green Peas

These are not-quite-scrambled eggs. "Broken" would be a better word; indeed, when you bring a carton of eggs home from the market and one has a broken shell, you refer to it as *escrachado*. I cook the eggs in a cast-iron skillet, stirring them just enough to break up the yolks a bit but leaving no doubt that there are separate white and yellow parts to an egg. Add cooked green vegetables and bacon, and you have what I would call a fine and delicious mess.

SERVES 4

2 small zucchini

4 ounces thickly sliced pancetta, cut into ½-inch cubes

1 tablespoon extra virgin olive oil

1 tablespoon unsalted butter

1 cup shelled baby peas

6 large eggs

Coarse salt and freshly ground black pepper

Trim the zucchini and slice lengthwise on a mandoline into very thin ribbons, laying them out on paper towels to keep them separate; pat them dry before cooking.

Sauté the pancetta in a cast-iron skillet over medium heat for about 5 minutes, turning occasionally, until crisp and lightly browned on all sides. Remove with a slotted spoon and drain on paper towels.

Wipe out the skillet and add the oil and butter. Heat until the butter melts, then add the zucchini ribbons and peas and cook for several minutes, until the zucchini softens and starts to brown. Turn to cook the other side for a minute or two.

Break the eggs into a bowl, then pour them into the skillet, pushing the vegetables around to make room and breaking the eggs up a bit as they begin to set. When the eggs are done to your liking, season them with salt and pepper and scatter the pancetta over the top. Serve immediately.

Tortilla of Cast-Iron Fried Potatoes, Spinach, and Sun-Dried Tomatoes

I cook each of the main ingredients separately and then bring them together at the end. That way, you get a more powerful statement of the essence of each one. The tortilla can be flipped or broiled for added browning; don't worry if it breaks. **SERVES 4**

2 Idaho (baking) potatoes, peeled
1 pound spinach, trimmed
½ cup extra virgin olive oil
8 tablespoons unsalted (1 stick) butter
    4 tablespoons cut into ½-inch pieces
Coarse salt and freshly ground black pepper
½ cup drained Sun-Dried Tomatoes (page 285)
12 large eggs
Double recipe Salsa Llajua (page 284)

Put the potatoes in a pot of cold water and bring to a boil over high heat. Reduce the heat to medium and boil gently for about 12 minutes, or until the potatoes are just tender enough to poke a skewer through them. Drain, pat dry on paper towels, and slice about ½ inch thick.

Meanwhile, blanch the spinach in a large pot of boiling water just until it wilts. Drain in a colander, cool under cold running water, and drain again, then squeeze very dry in a clean kitchen towel.

Heat ¼ cup of the olive oil and 2 tablespoons of the butter in a large cast-iron skillet over medium heat. Add half the potatoes and fry for about

4 minutes, until golden brown and crisp on the bottom. Turn and repeat on the other side. Transfer to a large plate and cook the second batch of potatoes, adding 2 more tablespoons each oil and butter; transfer to the plate. Season the potatoes with salt and pepper.

Reduce the heat under the skillet to medium-low and add the remaining 2 tablespoons olive oil. Add the sun-dried tomatoes, spreading them out in the pan. Arrange the fried potatoes on top, and distribute small clumps of the blanched spinach over the potatoes. Dot with the pieces of butter.

Beat the eggs lightly in a large bowl and season with salt and pepper. Pour one-third of the eggs over the potatoes and spinach, pulling in the edges as they set. Repeat with the remaining eggs in two batches, pulling in the edges as they set, and cook until the bottom is golden and the top is almost set, about 8 more minutes.

Run a spatula all around the edge of the pan to loosen the eggs, then set a wide plate over the top and invert the skillet to unmold the eggs onto the plate. Add more oil to the skillet and slide the eggs back in to finish cooking on the bottom. They are done when crisp and golden. Serve immediately, directly from the skillet, sliced into wedges, with the salsa on the side.

PICTURED ON PAGES 62 AND 66–67

Tortilla of Cast-Iron Fried Potatoes, Spinach, and Sun-Dried Tomatoes (page 65).

Tortilla of Prawns with Grilled Potatoes and Avocado, Chile Pepper, and Fennel Salsa

In recent years, I have grown fond of searing fish and shellfish on one side only, leaving the other side less cooked and more succulent and tender. This works particularly well with sweet fresh-caught shrimp, langoustines, and scallops, grilled and bound together with eggs.

Grilling thin slices of potato directly on a *parrilla* allows the smoke to permeate them in a way that captures the full aroma of a wood fire. If your grill is clean, they don't even need to be oiled. As the potatoes crisp, they will release from the grill grate and you can remove them easily. **SERVES 4**

FOR THE SALSA
1 ripe avocado
Juice of 1 lemon
1 ripe tomato, chopped
½ small red onion, chopped
½ fennel bulb, trimmed and chopped
1 red chile pepper, seeded and chopped
Extra virgin olive oil for drizzling

FOR THE TORTILLA
1 Idaho (baking) potato
8 ounces peeled prawns or large shrimp
About ¼ cup extra virgin olive oil
Coarse salt and freshly ground black pepper
6 large eggs
½ cup minced fresh flat-leaf parsley
1 or 2 green garlic stalks or garlic cloves, minced
1 onion, sliced very thin

To prepare the salsa, halve and pit the avocado. Scoop out and roughly chop the flesh, then toss it gently with the lemon juice in a bowl. Add the tomato, onion, fennel, and chile, drizzle with olive oil to taste, and toss to combine.

Heat a charcoal grill or two large cast-iron ridged grill pans over medium heat.

Slice the potato paper-thin on a mandoline; do not rinse or wipe the slices. Arrange them in rows on the grill or in the pans; work in batches if necessary. The grill marks on the bottom will become clearly visible from the top as they cook, and the potatoes will release themselves from the grill when they are ready to turn. Using tongs, turn each potato slice and grill on the other side until they are marked. As the potatoes are done, remove them with tongs and set aside in a bowl.

Brush the prawns and the grill grate or one grill pan with olive oil and season the prawns with salt and pepper. Grill the prawns on one side only for 2 to 3 minutes, until they are pink and crisp on the bottom. Remove them with tongs and transfer them to a separate bowl.

Break the eggs into a large bowl and beat lightly with a fork. Season to taste with salt and pepper, then whisk in the chopped parsley and minced garlic.

Heat 2 tablespoons of the oil in a well-seasoned 9-inch cast-iron skillet or a 9-inch nonstick skillet over medium heat. Sauté the sliced onion for about 7 minutes, until soft and translucent. Remove with a slotted spoon and fold into the egg mixture. Add the grilled potatoes, mixing them thoroughly into the eggs.

Add another tablespoon or so of olive oil to the skillet and, working quickly, arrange the shrimp, uncooked side down, in a circular pattern. Carefully pour the egg and potato mixture over the shrimp, taking care to disturb the arrangement as little as possible. Lower the heat a bit and cook gently for several minutes, lowering the heat again a bit if necessary, until the eggs are set and golden brown on the bottom; tilt the pan and lift the set eggs occasionally to allow the uncooked egg to flow to the bottom. When the eggs are almost set but still wet on top, cover the skillet with a large plate and, with your hand on the plate, in one quick motion, turn the skillet upside down to invert the tortilla onto the plate. Return the skillet to the heat, coat the bottom with more oil, and slide the tortilla back in to cook the other side for several minutes, until set on the bottom but still moist inside.

Slide the tortilla onto a clean platter and serve immediately, with the salsa on the side.

Asparagus Bundles Wrapped in Bacon with Fried Eggs

Bacon and eggs are a favorite breakfast, but these eggs fried with bundles of bacon-wrapped asparagus are also a superb lunch or supper. Serve with a green salad and country bread, washed down with a glass of rosé champagne. The thought would have horrified my grandmother, who believed, as many Europeans do, that eggs are not to be eaten in the evening. But a light supper like this is quick and easy and often hits just the right note.

This is best made with thin asparagus spears. If you use two griddles, make sure to cook some of the bacon-wrapped asparagus on each one, to flavor the eggs. **SERVES 4**

1 pound thin asparagus (16 to 20 spears)
4 slices best bacon
2 tablespoons extra virgin olive oil
2 tablespoons unsalted butter
8 large eggs
Lemon wedges
Crusty bread

Cut off the tough ends of the asparagus and trim them to an even length. Divide into 4 bundles. Wrap a slice of bacon around the center of each bundle and set aside, seam side down.

Heat a *chapa* or two large cast-iron griddles over medium heat. Brush with the oil. When it shimmers, arrange the bundles seam side down on the hot surface and cook for about 7 minutes. The bacon seams will close and some of the fat will render onto the griddle. If there is too much, mop some of it up with paper towels.

Turn the bundles, moving them to one side to make room for the eggs. Dot the hot surface with the butter, then lower the heat. When the butter melts, carefully break the eggs onto it and cook for about 5 minutes, until the whites have set but the yolks are still soft. The asparagus should be crunchy outside and tender within.

Divide the asparagus and eggs among four plates and serve with lemon wedges and sliced crusty bread.

Crisp Chicken Skin, Lettuce, and Heirloom Tomato Sandwich

In the 1980s, I came to New York to film a television show. One night we went to Chinatown, where I tasted Peking duck for the first time. The chef told me that the key to a great Peking duck is the crispy skin. As I thought about it, I realized that most people everywhere have the same affection for crispy chicken skin. Combining it as I do here with lettuce and tomato in a sandwich offers all the crispy, salty deliciousness of a BLT. So here, from China, by way of Manhattan and my Patagonian *chapa,* is a "CLT."

Ideally, the skin should be from a fresh-killed farm chicken, and preferably from the thighs. Cook it slowly over a medium-low fire, mopping up the fat as it renders, or it will get chewy instead of crisp.
SERVES 2

**2 Chapa Breads (page 268) or other sandwich
    rolls, split**
Skin from 2 large chicken thighs
Extra virgin olive oil
Coarse sea salt
2 small heirloom tomatoes, cut in half
¼ cup Basil Aioli (recipe follows)
2 crisp lettuce leaves

Heat a *chapa* or a large cast-iron skillet over medium-low heat. Set the buns cut side down on the hot surface for a minute or so to toast. Transfer to serving plates.

Pat the chicken skin dry with paper towels and cut it into rough 2-inch pieces. Brush the *chapa* with olive oil. When the oil shimmers, add the chicken skin, fatty side down, season with salt, and cook slowly for several minutes, until the fat renders out and the skin is crisp and golden brown. Turn and repeat on the other side.

While the chicken skin is cooking, brush the cut sides of the tomatoes with olive oil and add them to the *chapa.* Cook, without moving them, for about 4 minutes, until the bottom is nicely charred.

Spread each cut side of the toasted buns with a tablespoon of aioli. Arrange the lettuce and charred tomatoes on the bottom halves, top with the chicken skin, and close the sandwiches. Serve immediately.

Basil Aioli

Serve with grilled fish or use in other sandwiches. The basic aioli can be made a few hours ahead and refrigerated, but to preserve its bright color, slice the basil and stir it in just before serving.
MAKES ABOUT 1 CUP

2 large egg yolks, at room temperature
1 garlic clove, peeled
Coarse salt
¾ cup extra virgin olive oil
1 teaspoon fresh lemon juice
1 cup fresh basil leaves

Place the egg yolks in a bowl and grate the garlic over them with a Microplane. Season with a pinch of salt. Add about ¼ cup of the olive oil to the egg yolks a few drops at a time, whisking constantly until the mixture emulsifies. Then add the remaining olive oil in a slow, steady stream, whisking constantly, until the aioli is a thick and shiny mass. Whisk in the lemon juice. Cover and refrigerate until ready to use.

Just before using, slice the basil into a fine chiffonade and stir into the aioli.

Grilled Skirt Steak Sandwich with Watercress, Onion, Tomato, and Mustard

Skirt steak is very much a gaucho favorite. Our roughneck Argentinean cowboys often stand around a fire while the meat cooks, and then they will cut off a piece of bread and a slice of meat with their knives to eat while standing up. This particular sandwich, which I first made under the Brooklyn Bridge, is as close as most people will get to a fireside meal on the pampas. Strong English mustard livens up the palate and the sourdough and tomatoes add some acidity that cuts through the fat, although a gaucho would have no time for such fanciness as mustard and vegetables. SERVES 4

4 crusty sourdough sandwich rolls, split
Colman's English mustard or other strong mustard
1½ pounds skirt steak
Coarse salt and freshly ground black pepper
2 ripe tomatoes, sliced
1 bunch watercress, trimmed, rinsed, and dried
1 red onion, thinly sliced
Extra virgin olive oil for drizzling

Heat a charcoal grill or a large ridged cast-iron grill pan over high heat. Set the sourdough rolls cut side down on the hot surface for a minute or so to toast. When they are nicely marked, remove and spread both cut sides generously with mustard. Set aside.

Pat the steak dry with paper towels. (If the steak is too long for your grill pan, cut it in half.) Sprinkle one side of the meat with salt, set salted side down on the grill or pan, and cook for about 2 minutes, until nicely marked but still rare. Season with salt and pepper, turn the meat, and grill for 1 to 2 minutes more—it should still be quite rare when you cut into it. Transfer to a cutting board and slice across the grain.

Layer the steak, tomatoes, watercress, and onions in the rolls. Season with salt and pepper, drizzle with olive oil, and serve immediately.

OPPOSITE: Cooking in the morning under the Brooklyn Bridge.

Tuna Churrasco and Avocado Sandwich

In Argentina, a *churrasco* is a thin steak cooked quickly. Here I use tuna instead of beef. The avocado adds richness and creaminess and makes it taste like a tuna-avocado roll in a sushi restaurant. I toss the sliced avocado with fresh lemon juice, and the result is a bright accompaniment to the barely cooked tuna.

Many people have strong negative opinions about cilantro—and usually I am one of them. Like many chefs trained in the French tradition, I don't love it. But I am also open to trying new things, and I discovered it works beautifully here. **SERVES 4**

1 large ripe avocado
Juice of 1 large lemon
One 1-pound fresh yellowfin tuna steak, sliced
½ inch thick
Extra virgin olive oil
4 Chapa Breads (page 268) or other sandwich
rolls, split
20 fresh cilantro leaves
Coarse salt and freshly ground black pepper

Heat a *chapa* or a large cast-iron griddle over very high heat. Meanwhile, cut the avocado in half and remove the pit. Scoop out the flesh neatly and slice ½ inch thick. Toss with the lemon juice and set aside.

Pat the tuna dry with paper towels. Brush the hot surface of the *chapa* with olive oil, and when it shimmers, add the tuna. Cook on one side only for about 1 minute, until the bottom begins to brown but the tuna is still raw on top.

Cover the bottom of each bun with some tuna and then add 5 cilantro leaves. Season with salt and pepper, drizzle with olive oil, and top with the sliced avocado. Add the tops of the buns and serve immediately.

Open-Faced Pomegranate Jelly and Lardo Sandwich

When I was a young boy, we lived outside Chicago for a few years in the town of Naperville (my dad was working as a physicist with the Atomic Energy Commission). Like all kids, I loved peanut butter and jelly sandwiches. The combination of the nutty creaminess of peanut butter and the sweetness of jelly is what led me to conceive of this "grown-up" idea. Lardo is supercreamy, and pomegranate jelly is sweet; however, the fresh pomegranate seeds are quite tangy, cutting through both the fat and the sweetness. The burnt crust of the country bread does the same. **MAKES 4 OPEN-FACED SANDWICHES**

1 pomegranate
8 thin slices lardo
4 pieces Ember-Toasted Bread (page 290), still
      warm
Pomegranate jelly

Cut the pomegranate in half and shake the seeds out into a bowl.

Arrange 2 lardo slices on each piece of bread; it should begin to melt. Spoon a teaspoonful or two of pomegranate jelly down the center of the lardo on each piece. Sprinkle with some pomegranate seeds, and serve immediately.

LA RUTA AZUL,
PATAGONIA

La Ruta Azul—the Blue Highway—
hugs the windswept Atlantic Coast
of Patagonia. It runs through the
provinces of Chubut and Santa Cruz,
which end their long descent here,
one that begins in the glaciers of the
Andean highlands and traverses the
grassy pampas to this desolate yet
beautiful shore.

It has always been far from
everywhere. Only the heartiest people
have settled here and stayed. Many
more moved on to richer, more fertile
lands to the west. In olden times,
people made a living harvesting
seaweed or melting the fat derived
from sea lions and seals. It is a harsh
land, with many shipwrecks offshore.
The people here remind me of
those hearty folk along the coast of
Ireland, or on the islands off Scotland,
somehow wresting a livelihood from
cold waters and barren land. The
creatures of the sea, however, don't
know that it is such a brutal place.
For them it is rich, teeming with life.
All kinds of fish, shellfish, and sea

mammals inhabit its waters and shorelines. This is the only place on earth where right whales come to mate. Do you know why the American seafarers who hunted them to the brink of extinction called them right whales? Because they were just right for getting the most whale oil. How unfortunate for the whales.

Years ago, if I drove through this land at all, I followed the main road ten miles inland, giving little thought to the magic of the sea. But then one winter, I made a pilgrimage along the coast to visit all the abandoned lighthouses that once stood as sentinels, warning mariners to steer clear of the treacherous, fog-bound coast. We slept outside in sleeping bags even though it was 10 degrees Celsius (low 40s Fahrenheit). When you are young, the romance of such journeys keeps you warm, or at least unmindful of the chill.

I had always wanted to return to this land of desolate beauty, and so one summer (even then not all that warm), I built myself a cook's cabin by the shore. I went each day to the harbor of Bahía Bustamente and befriended the fishermen there. Every day they returned with fish in many different varieties, and every evening I would build a fire. When it spoke to me, I cooked something new.

BEEF, LAMB, AND PORK

Veal Rib Chops and French Green Beans a la Plancha with Romaine-Watercress Salad

This is not a Patagonian dish—we don't have white milk-fed veal in Argentina, where all our cattle graze on wild grasses. So it is always tempting for me when I am in a country where veal is prized to prepare some. Veal chops need plenty of space around them to brown well. Make sure to leave at least a good inch all around each chop. If you crowd them together, they will steam instead of developing a beautiful caramelized crust on the outside. Once they are browned, the green beans are added to the *chapa* to pick up some of the garlicky juices. Prepare the salad before you start cooking, but do not dress it until just before serving.

I sometimes wonder why people don't use salsify more. Eaten raw, it has refreshing crunch and a hint of pungency. Watercress is bracingly peppery, and romaine, the most-full-bodied lettuce, doesn't get lost among the other strong flavors and textures. With a red wine vinaigrette, this is a side salad that works well with many grilled meats. I'll just note here that all the great French chefs of the nineteenth century served watercress alongside meat, so this is a bit of an homage to them. SERVES 4

FOR THE SALAD
1 large garlic clove, minced
2 tablespoons red wine vinegar
5 tablespoons extra virgin olive oil
1 large salsify root
Coarse salt and freshly ground black pepper
1 head romaine
1 bunch watercress, tough stems removed, rinsed, and dried

FOR THE VEAL
6 garlic cloves, smashed and chopped
4 thick veal rib chops, about
    12 ounces each, preferably bone-in

Coarse salt and freshly ground black pepper
About 3 tablespoons extra virgin olive oil
12 ounces French green beans (haricots verts), topped and tailed
2 tablespoons unsalted butter, cut into small pieces
Grated zest of 1 lemon
Pinch of freshly grated nutmeg

To make the salad, whisk the garlic and vinegar together in a small bowl. Gradually whisk in the olive oil until emulsified. Peel the salsify and cut into rough julienne strips. Immediately add it to the vinaigrette, tossing to coat well to prevent darkening. Season with salt and pepper.

Tear the romaine and watercress into bite-size pieces and place in a wide serving bowl.

To make the chops, heat a *chapa* or two large cast-iron griddles over medium heat. Scatter the chopped garlic over both sides of the veal chops and rub it into the meat, tucking it into any crevices. Season with salt and pepper.

Brush the hot surface of the *chapa* generously with oil. When the oil shimmers, add the veal chops (if you are using two griddles, put 2 chops on each) and cook, without moving them, for 6 minutes, or until seared and browned on the bottom. When the chops are almost ready to turn, arrange the green beans around them and dot them with the butter; turn the beans too as they soften and brown. Turn the chops and cook for 4 minutes, or until browned on the second side but still slightly pink inside when cut into. Transfer the chops to a platter, sprinkle with the lemon zest, and let rest for 3 minutes.

Meanwhile, when the beans are cooked, season with salt, pepper, and the nutmeg and turn them around in the juices. Transfer to the platter with the chops. Just before serving, add the salsify vinaigrette to the greens and toss to combine. Adjust the seasoning and serve.

Albondigas with Lentils

During my boyhood in Bariloche, when the snow piled up and the wind whipped down off the high Andes, these meatballs were the delight of the Mallmann boys. You needed something hearty to fuel you for skiing, sledding, and making snowmen. The Spanish word for meatballs is *albondigas*. It's such a fun word to say; when we were little, we would drive our mom a bit crazy as we chanted it over and over. No matter what you call them, kids everywhere love meatballs. Getting a good crust on them is important. And make sure the meat is not too lean—70% lean, 30% fat makes juicy meatballs. **SERVES 4**

FOR THE LENTILS
About 1 tablespoon extra virgin olive oil
3 ounces pancetta, chopped
2 medium onions, chopped
3 garlic cloves, thinly sliced
1 large portobello cap, quartered (if large) and sliced ⅓ inch thick
1 cup dry red wine
1 pound ripe plum tomatoes, chopped
8 ounces du Puy lentils
8 fresh thyme sprigs, tied together with kitchen string
3 cups Rich Vegetable Stock (page 288)
Coarse salt and freshly ground black pepper

FOR THE MEATBALLS
8 ounces ground pork (70% lean)
8 ounces ground beef (70% lean)
1 tablespoon red wine vinegar
1½ tablespoons Dijon mustard
2 garlic cloves, grated or finely minced
¼ cup packed fresh basil leaves, sliced
¼ cup minced fresh chives
3 tablespoons minced fresh flat-leaf parsley
¾ teaspoon crushed red pepper flakes
1 large egg, lightly beaten
1 tablespoon extra virgin olive oil

FOR SERVING
Grilled bread
Cubed heirloom tomatoes
Diced red onion

To make the lentils, heat the olive oil in a deep heavy pot over medium heat. Add the pancetta, onions, and garlic and sauté until the pancetta renders its fat and the onions are softened. Add the mushroom, red wine, tomatoes, lentils, and thyme, bring to a boil, and let bubble for a couple of minutes to reduce the wine and let the vegetables absorb its flavor. Add the stock and bring to a boil, then lower the heat and simmer for about 40 minutes, until the lentils are tender. The mixture should be soupy; if necessary, add some water. Season to taste with salt and pepper.

Meanwhile, make the meatballs: Combine the ground meat, vinegar, mustard, garlic, basil, chives, parsley, and red pepper flakes in a bowl and mix well with your hands or a wooden spoon. Mix in the egg. Shape the mixture into 12 meatballs.

Brush a large cast-iron skillet with the oil and heat over medium-high heat until it shimmers. Add the meatballs, in batches if necessary, giving them plenty of space to brown, and cook until browned on the first side, about 3 minutes. Turn and brown the other side. Transfer the meatballs to a plate as they are done and set aside.

When the lentils are done, add them to the same skillet and bring to a low bubble, scraping up any caramelized juices on the bottom of the pan and stirring to combine. Nestle the meatballs in the lentils and simmer until they are cooked through, about 15 minutes. If the lentils become dry, add a little water.

Serve with grilled bread, tomatoes, and onions.

Cowboy Rib Eye a la Plancha with Crispy Brioche Salad and Grilled Dates

I first learned the technique of pan-roasting rib eye when I apprenticed in France. Before that, I had always cooked steak on a grill over an open fire. But you can get a gorgeous crunchy crust with a luscious pink interior using a cast-iron skillet or a *chapa*. When I dreamed up this recipe on the shores of Red Hook, we were in sight of the Statue of Liberty, a gift from the French people to the United States, so I felt duty bound to include a French touch—and decided to toast some brioche on the *chapa*. Toast wants something sweet on it, so onto the *chapa* as well went some dates and, for contrast and piquancy, some arugula. **SERVES 2 OR 3**

One 2-inch-thick bone-in rib-eye steak, about 2 pounds

About ⅓ cup extra virgin olive oil

Fleur de sel

1 small brioche loaf (about 6 ounces), crusts trimmed off, torn into rough ½-inch pieces (about 2 cups)

½ cup Dijon mustard

Freshly ground black pepper

½ teaspoon crushed red pepper flakes, or to taste

4 large, soft fresh dates, such as Medjool, pitted and spread open

1 bunch arugula, tough stems removed

Heat a *chapa* or a cast-iron griddle over medium heat. Pat the steak dry with paper towels. Brush the *chapa* generously with olive oil. When the oil shimmers, sprinkle one side of the steak with fleur de sel and set it salt side down on the hot surface. After about 10 minutes, when the steak is browned and crusty on the bottom, season the top with salt and flip it over to cook on the other side for about 8 more minutes, or until nicely browned. Stand the steak upright on its side to brown the fat for several minutes, then lay it back down and cook on each side for a minute or two, until the internal temperature reaches 120°F for rare. Transfer it to a carving board and let it rest for 10 minutes while you make the brioche salad. (The temperature will increase slightly as it rests.)

Add a tablespoon of olive oil to the pan drippings. Arrange the pieces of brioche on the hot surface to toast: this can take less than a minute, depending on the heat of the *chapa,* so keep your eye on them and turn them before they burn. As the bread is toasting, dot it all over with the mustard, and season with salt, black pepper, and the red pepper flakes. Drizzle olive oil generously over it, then fit the dates in, cut side down. Scatter the arugula over the top and, using two spatulas, toss it all together as you would a salad, scraping up the drippings, oil, and mustard to combine. Sprinkle the salad generously with olive oil and heap it on a serving platter.

Slice the meat, season with salt and pepper, and drizzle with olive oil. Serve with the salad, spooning the juices over all.

Côte de Bœuf a la Parrilla with Maître d'Hôtel Butter

People say you can judge a restaurant by its roast chicken. Equally true for me, you can tell a lot about the quality of a nation's beef by the beauty of its rib-eye steak. It's a luxurious cut, shot through with succulent fat that makes it tender. In France, I used my Argentine grill to cook a côte de bœuf from their wonderful Charolais cattle, huge beasts with meat that is almost purple. Maître d'hôtel butter, which I learned to make during my first French apprenticeship, is nothing more than a mix of butter, parsley, and lemon. You might ask why a fatty cut like a côte de bœuf would need more fat. You will have your answer when you taste this. **SERVES 2**

FOR THE MAÎTRE D'HÔTEL BUTTER
4 tablespoons unsalted butter, at room temperature
1 teaspoon minced fresh thyme
2 tablespoons minced fresh flat-leaf parsley
1 tablespoon fresh lemon juice

A bunch of thyme

2 strips lemon zest
Coarse salt and freshly ground black pepper
¼ cup extra virgin olive oil
¼ cup medium-bodied red wine
One 1½- to 2-pound 1½-inch-thick bone-in
   rib-eye steak

Heat a charcoal grill or a deep-ridged cast-iron grill pan over medium heat.

To make the maître d'hôtel butter, put the butter in a small bowl, add the minced thyme, parsley, and lemon juice, and mix together with a fork until well combined. Turn out onto a length of plastic wrap and, using the plastic to help you, form into a log about 1 inch thick. Chill to firm.

Tie the thyme sprigs together with kitchen twine to use as a basting brush.

Whisk together the lemon zest, salt and pepper to taste, olive oil, and red wine in a bowl. This will be your basting liquid.

When the cooking surface is hot, salt one side of the meat, put it salt side down on the grill, and cook, without moving it, for 5 minutes. Baste the top, then rotate the meat a quarter turn to form crosshatched grill marks. Baste the top again. Grill for 4 minutes, or until nicely marked, then salt the meat, flip it over, and repeat. When the internal temperature reads 120°F, the steak will be rare (it will rise a few degrees as it rests). If you prefer it a little more cooked, give it another minute or two.

Meanwhile, slice the chilled herb butter into disks.

When the meat is done to your taste, transfer it to a carving board, with some disks of herb butter beneath it and the rest on top. Let the meat rest for 5 minutes before carving. Serve with the buttery juices.

Grilled Short Ribs
with Vinegar-Glazed Charred Endive

In Europe and America, short ribs are most often braised until the meat is very soft and falls off the bone at the slightest touch. Argentines like them grilled and more chewy but still well-done, with a salty, crunchy crust. I like the crust but I prefer my ribs medium-rare, which is quite easy to achieve on a *chapa*. Argentine cooks prefer cross-cut ribs, but when cut English style, the ribs make a dramatic carnivorous statement. When I prepared these in Bushwick, Brooklyn, in front of the popular restaurant Roberta's, I dressed some endive leaves with vinaigrette and threw them on the very hot griddle for a minute so that they softened a bit. The bitter green was as piquant as Patagonian chimichurri and cut the fattiness of the meat perfectly. **SERVES 4**

4 pounds English-cut beef short ribs, trimmed of tough pieces of fell (papery membrane) and excess fat
Coarse salt and freshly ground black pepper
2 tablespoons Dijon mustard, plus more for serving
¼ cup red wine vinegar
2 tablespoons extra virgin olive oil
4 endives, leaves separated
Extra virgin olive oil for drizzling

Heat a *chapa* or a large cast-iron griddle over medium-high heat. Pat the short ribs completely dry with paper towels. Season them on one side with salt and pepper. Place seasoned side down on the hot surface and cook, without moving the ribs, for about 8 minutes, or until a crunchy brown crust forms on the bottom. Sprinkle the other side with salt and pepper, turn, and brown, basting the tops with a bit of the fat if they look dry at any time. If there is a lot of fat, mop most of it up with paper towels—you want the ribs to sear, not fry.

Meanwhile, whisk together the mustard and 2 tablespoons of the vinegar in a large bowl, then gradually whisk in the olive oil. Season with salt and pepper. Add the endive and toss to coat with the dressing.

When the ribs are browned on all sides, check the temperature with an instant-read thermometer. If they are not yet at 140°F, move them to a cooler part of the *chapa* (or lower the heat under the griddle) and continue cooking them, turning every 5 minutes or so and checking the temperature, until they are done. Transfer them to a platter.

Deglaze the hot cooking surface with the remaining 2 tablespoons vinegar, scraping up the bits of beef and caramelized juices. If using a griddle, raise the heat to very high. Arrange the endive leaves rounded side up on the hot surface and cook for several minutes, until nicely charred. Use one or two wide spatulas to scrape up the endive and any remaining deglazing liquid and transfer to the platter with the ribs. Drizzle with olive oil and serve with mustard on the side.

Anytime, Anywhere

A warm, sunny late afternoon. The light throws a cloak of gold over the waning day. A glass of wine turns the scene even lovelier and conversation more congenial. These are the things that come to mind when you think of a perfect barbecue. Picture it, as I do now, in a meadow by a sun-dappled chestnut grove, with the sound of a burbling stream as background music. But such days should not be the only time you cook out of doors. Cold days, windy days, snowy days, rainy days, dark and cloudy days all have their charms and challenges to the builder of fires and the griller of food: a barren winter hillside with the sun lighting up a halo of windswept snow. A makeshift canopy by a lake shore as dark clouds, pregnant with rain, bear down. An abandoned churchyard in a high-desert ghost town, with the walls of the ruined chapel as a windbreak. A cobbled Brooklyn street, where I am sure Walt Whitman once came to stare at the waterfront. All perfectly suited to my traveling Patagonian grill. So, too, a Parisian cul-de-sac in misting rain in Saint-Germain-des-Prés. A parking lot by a Buenos Aires soccer field on a sweltering summer day. A friend's yard on the shores of Lake Nahuel Huapi, near my Patagonian hometown.

Many chefs take pride and pleasure in making a meal with whatever ingredients are at hand. I am that way with fire and weather. Whatever weather the gods hurl my way, as long as I have wood or charcoal, a place to kindle a flame, and some way to expose ingredients to the heat of the fire, I know I can make a fine meal. You certainly don't need an expensive barbecue grill that looks like the command console of a space station. A simple grate propped up with rocks over a fire on the ground is all that fifteen generations of gauchos have used to turn out their grilled masterpieces. Or cook with fires between flat rocks the way the Incas and their Nazca ancestors did for thousands of years. The Indians of Patagonia even grilled over fires in canoes! A sharpened sapling used to impale fresh-caught fish and then set next to a campfire fed Indians on the Guarani River for centuries in the high Andes. I never stop learning: a taxi driver who took me to the airport in Buenos Aires suggested wrapping a stuffed fish in brown paper and throwing it on the grill. I made a note to try it as soon as I could. The saying may be "Where there is smoke, there is fire," but my heart tells me something else. Wherever and whenever you can make a fire, you can make a meal.

OPPOSITE: By the old iron bridge in Garzón. When you have a portable grill, you can cook anywhere.

Sliced Kidney Strips a la Plancha with Salsa Provenzal

The British are fond of what they call the "nasty bits," or offal. In the United States, these are not as popular.

The most important thing when cooking kidneys is to make sure you give them ample space; if you crowd them, they will steam and become chewy. And cook them only briefly, just until they cease sizzling after you've added them to the pan. Then turn and, again, cook until the sizzle quiets down. This will give you a crunchy outside and a perfectly done interior. If you want them more well-done, transfer the kidneys to a colander to drain, then repeat the sizzle in a pan with fresh butter. For well-done, do it three times. The only thing you don't want to do is to cook very long past the sizzle.

This is an adaptation of a recipe I made in the classic French kitchen at Le Grand Véfour, when I was young and still immersed in learning haute cuisine. Argentine salsa provenzal makes a lighter dish than the heavy cream-laden affair on traditional menus. Serve with Tortilla of Cast-Iron Potatoes, Spinach, and Sun-Dried Tomatoes (page 65).

SERVES 4

1 pound veal kidneys, carefully trimmed of fat
6 tablespoons unsalted butter
Double recipe Salsa Provenzal (page 284)

Slice the kidneys across the lobes into long strips about ¼ inch thick; remove any remaining fat. Pat the strips dry with paper towels.

Heat a large cast-iron skillet over medium-high heat and add half the butter. When it hisses and foams, add the kidney strips, without crowding them (cook in batches if necessary), and cook, without moving them, for just a minute or two, until they have just stopped sizzling and are browned on the bottom. Spoon some of the salsa over them, add the rest of the butter to the skillet, and turn the strips. They will be done in another minute or two.

Serve with the remaining salsa on the side.

Calves' Liver a la Plancha with Pimentón Oil, Onions, and Crunchy Potatoes

I find the mineralized flavor of liver particularly pleasing. Here I use an oil infused with sweet pimentón de Murcia for the liver and one with rosemary for the potatoes and onions. Liver and onions is a Venetian classic, and this dish, with the onions done in an *horno,* is my variation on that theme. **SERVES 4**

4 Idaho (baking) potatoes, scrubbed
5 tablespoons rosemary oil (see page 281),
    at room temperature
Course sea salt, such as Maldon or fleur de sel,
    and freshly ground black pepper
2 red onions, sliced
¼ cup Pimentón Oil (page 281)
1½ pounds calves' liver, trimmed and sliced about
    ½ inch thick
Olive oil for brushing

Heat an *horno* or the oven to 375°F, with a rack in the lower third. Set two 8- or 9-inch cast-iron skillets on the rack to preheat for about 10 minutes.

Meanwhile, cover the potatoes with water in a large saucepan and bring to a boil. Reduce the heat to a low boil and cook gently until the potatoes are tender, about 15 minutes. Drain, pat dry on paper towels, and break into halves or quarters.

Remove one skillet from the oven, coat the bottom with some of the rosemary oil, and arrange the potatoes in it. They should pile up in an attractive heap. Drizzle with half the remaining rosemary oil and season with salt and pepper. Bake for about 15 minutes, or until the potatoes are golden brown and crunchy on the outside.

Meanwhile, toss the onion slices with the remaining rosemary oil to coat. Arrange in the second cast-iron skillet and cook in the oven for about 15 minutes, turning them over halfway through, until they are softened and nicely caramelized.

While the potatoes and onions are browning, spoon the pimentón oil onto a plate and turn the liver slices in it to coat both sides. Season well with coarse sea salt.

Heat a *chapa* or a large cast-iron griddle over medium-high heat for 10 minutes. Brush the surface with olive oil. When the oil shimmers, add the liver slices, spaced well apart (cook in batches if necessary), and cook for 1 to 2 minutes, until browned and crusty on the bottom. Baste the top with pimentón oil, turn the liver, and cook for another minute or so, until done to taste; it should still be quite pink inside.

Serve immediately, with the onions and potatoes.

PAGE 106: Crunchy potatoes roasted in the oven. **PAGE 107:** Spooning pimentón oil over the calves' liver on the *chapa.*

Weeping Lamb

When I say this lamb weeps, I am talking about the way the fat drips onto the vegetables below and crisps them. This dish orginated in the Malvinas, the islands due east of Chubut in the South Atlantic. The British, who have claimed them, call them the Falklands, but no self-respecting Argentine would. *"Las Malvinas son Argentinas,"* we say. Although I have never attempted a conversation with a Malvinas lamb, the word "weeping" is particularly apt because I think the sheep are sad that they are not Argentine.

The lamb is first slow-roasted to render most of the fat, then set on a rack over the vegetables and crisped at higher heat. The vegetables pick up enough of the remaining fat to imbue them with richness and flavor. Serve with plenty of napkins!

SERVES 4

12 garlic cloves, peeled
8 fresh thyme sprigs
4 pounds bone-in breast of lamb (also called lamb
    riblets), cut into 4 racks
Coarse salt and freshly ground black pepper
2 red bell peppers
4 large red potatoes, peeled
2 onions, sliced
2 leeks, white part only, sliced
2 tablespoons extra virgin olive oil

Heat an *horno* or the oven to 325°F, with a rack in the lower third.

Cut 4 of the garlic cloves into slivers. Tear the thyme sprigs into small pieces. Cut small slits in the meat in between the bones and insert a garlic sliver and a piece of thyme into each. Reserve the extra thyme.

Season the lamb generously with salt and pepper and place fat side down in a large roasting pan. Cover tightly with foil and roast for 1½ hours, or until tender; check it every 20 or 30 minutes and pour off most of the fat as it accumulates.

Meanwhile, core and seed the peppers and cut them lengthwise into ½-inch-wide strips. Slice the potatoes about ⅓ inch thick. Toss the peppers, potatoes, onions, and leeks together in a bowl with the olive oil, salt and pepper to taste, the reserved thyme, and the remaining garlic cloves.

When the lamb is completely tender, remove it from the oven and raise the heat to 425°F. Remove the lamb from the pan and pour off all but 2 tablespoons of the fat, then arrange the vegetables in the pan. Set a rack over the vegetables, set the lamb fat side up on the rack, and roast, uncovered, for about 30 minutes longer, carefully lifting the lamb so you can turn the vegetables halfway through.

When the lamb is browned and crisp and the vegetables are tender, remove from the oven, arrange on a large platter, and serve immediately.

Leg of Lamb on Strings
with Mint-Chile Salmuera

If you like rotisserie cooking but don't have a rotisserie, here is a low-tech alternative. Hanging a leg of lamb or a whole chicken (or both) from a high tree branch with butcher's twine over a fire works perfectly. I first tried this at my little restaurant in Trancoso (see pages 233–239), and I was quite pleased with my new invention. Then Peter Kaminsky told me that he had once seen the same method used by a Masai cook in the Serengeti, where the result is known as "poacher's lamb." He said the man was an A-1 chef, so I wasn't disappointed to learn that the same inspiration had visited another lover of wood-fire cookery.

If you have a high, sturdy tree branch at least 10 feet above your grill that extends far enough from the tree itself to prevent it from being harmed by the fire, climb up a tall ladder and loop double lengths of heavy twine over the branch, with enough left over to truss the lamb and chicken. If you don't have such a tree, you will need to rig a sturdy iron or steel stand to hang the meat so that it will be about 2 feet above the fire.

Use a double thickness of butcher's twine or food-grade stainless steel wire to tie up the lamb, configuring loops on the sides and ends for hanging them. Turn occasionally as they cook, and raise or lower them as necessary. **SERVES 8 TO 10**

1 semi-boneless leg of lamb, about 7 pounds
Coarse salt and freshly ground black pepper
Mint-Chile Salmuera (page 287)

Build your fire and rake the coals out for medium heat.

Season the lamb with salt and pepper. If desired, brown it on all sides on an oiled grate over the fire before hanging it from the tree or metal stand.

Truss the lamb securely with butcher's twine or wire. Attach the lamb securely to the twine or wire at the end of the shank bone so it is suspended butt end down about 2 feet over the coals. The lamb will be done in about 3½ hours—the internal temperature should read 135°F for medium-rare. Let it rest for 15 minutes before carving. Keep in mind that some parts will be more done than others, so you can serve your guests to their taste.

Arrange the lamb on a platter and serve the salmuera on the side.

VARIATION:
Chicken on Strings
Suspend a trussed, 4-pound, farm-raised chicken and cook over fire. The chicken will be done in about 2 hours—an instant-read thermometer inserted in the thickest part of the thigh should read 160°F. Let it rest for 5 minutes before carving.

PICTURED ON PAGES 110–111

Leg of Lamb with Merguez, Coal-Roasted Delicata Squash, and Orange, Black Pepper, and Rosemary Salmuera

Throw some sausages on the grill just before your leg of lamb is done. Merguez sausages are super-savory and let your palate know "Here comes a meal that makes a strong statement." The full-flavored lamb really cries out for a vegetable to calm its rowdy effect. I first came across delicata squash in a farmers' market in Bolinas. It was new to me, and I became an instant convert.

I placed the squash on top of live coals: no grill, no grate, no *plancha*. I have become quite fond of cooking this way, letting the ingredients commune with fire without any interference. If I fan the coals before adding the food, I don't have to worry about it picking up any ashes. The orange-rosemary salmuera complements both the lamb and the squash. **SERVES 8**

1 semi-boneless leg of lamb, about 6 pounds
8 garlic cloves, slivered
4 fresh rosemary sprigs, broken into small pieces
4 fresh thyme sprigs, broken into small pieces
Coarse sea salt and freshly ground black pepper
Extra virgin olive oil
1 pound merguez or other lamb sausages
3 pounds delicata squash
Orange, Black Pepper, and Rosemary Salmuera
   (page 287)

Prepare a low fire in a charcoal grill.

With a small sharp knife, make small evenly spaced incisions on all sides of the lamb. Stuff the incisions with the garlic, rosemary, and thyme, alternating them as you go. Season well with salt and pepper and brush with olive oil. Oil the grill grate, place the lamb on the grate, and grill for about 2½ hours, turning occasionally, until done to taste; an instant-read thermometer will register 135°F for medium-rare.

When the lamb is almost done, prick the sausages in several places so they don't burst and add them to the grill. Turn them as they brown; they will take about 15 minutes or so to cook through, depending on the thickness.

When the lamb is done, transfer it to a carving board and let it rest for 15 minutes.

Meanwhile, cut the squash lengthwise in half and remove the seeds. Set directly on the coals, skin side down, and cook for several minutes, just until it is lightly charred. Turn and briefly char the cut side. Then remove with tongs, set skin side down on the grill with the sausages, and grill, basting occasionally with olive oil, until the flesh is tender to the center when pierced with a skewer—the timing will vary depending on the size and maturity of the squash.

Carve the lamb and serve with the sausages and thick slices of grilled squash, with the salmuera on the side.

PRECEDING: Lamb and chickens suspended over a fire. For the chicken, I used rebar from a construction site. The meat receives very even heat, and you can control the amount of heat by raising or lowering the lengths of twine.

Butterflied Leg of Lamb with Rosemary and Thyme and Charred Apple Salsa

Sweet apples and the perfume of fresh thyme play well against the bold aromas and flavor of grilled lamb. The mistake that people often make with butterflied lamb is to treat it like a porterhouse steak and cook it over a hot fire, with a black-and-blue result (burnt on the outside, raw on the inside). Take your time. Slower is almost always better, and if you want more of a crust, give it a blast over hot coals at the end. As with all big cuts of meat, it is a good idea to use an instant-read thermometer. If you like it rosy, take it from the heat at 135°F and let it rest for 10 minutes. **SERVES 6**

FOR THE LAMB
1 butterflied leg of lamb, about 3 pounds
1 tablespoon extra virgin olive oil, plus
    more if using a grill pan
Sea salt and freshly ground black pepper
2 tablespoons fresh thyme leaves
1 tablespoon fresh rosemary leaves
Grated zest of 1 lemon

FOR THE SALSA
1 cup extra virgin olive oil
3 large shallots, sliced
4 garlic cloves, very finely chopped
2 Granny Smith apples
2 tablespoons red wine vinegar
Coarse salt and freshly ground black pepper

Open the lamb out on a work surface. Brush with the olive oil and season liberally with salt and pepper. Scatter the thyme and rosemary leaves evenly over the top of the meat and pat them down firmly to make them adhere.

Heat a charcoal grill or a deep-ridged two-burner cast-iron grill pan over medium-low heat. If using a grill pan, brush it well with oil and heat until it shimmers. Carefully turn the lamb onto the grill or pan, herb side down, and cook very slowly for about 40 minutes, or until the bottom is crisp and brown.

Meanwhile, prepare the salsa: Heat a tablespoon or so of the oil in a large cast-iron skillet over medium-low heat. Add the shallots and garlic and cook, stirring occasionally, until caramelized, about 10 minutes. Transfer to a small bowl.

While the shallots and garlic are cooking, peel the apples so there is a bit of fruit attached to the skin, and tear the peel into rough 2-inch pieces. Reserve the apples for another use.

Wipe out the skillet, raise the heat to high, and heat for a few minutes. When the pan is extremely hot, add the strips of apple peel, skin side down, and let them char slowly, without moving them, for 4 minutes, or until they are about half charred.

Transfer the apples to a board and coarsely chop. Add the charred apple to the shallots and garlic. Stir in the red wine vinegar and then the remaining olive oil, and season to taste with salt and pepper. Set aside.

Turn the meat and grill the other side for about 20 minutes more, until it is browned and crisp on the second side and the internal temperature in the thickest part reads 135°F. (The temperature will rise to 140°F or so as the meat rests.) Transfer to a carving board, sprinkle with the grated lemon zest, and let rest for at least 10 minutes.

Carve the lamb at the table and serve with the charred apple salsa.

Parrillada of Pork and Vegetables

In the United States, cooking a whole hog is a spectacle at a meal for big events. This is a similar idea, except I've downsized it for 18 people with about a quarter of a pig rather than a whole one. It is broken down into separate cuts so that each can get the proper cooking time and develop a delicious crust. If the neighbors complain, invite them over. If the fire department complains, invite them too.

This is a long affair, and no doubt some of your grilling-enthusiast friends will want to be there for the whole event. Sausages cook quickly, so they are great to throw on the grill and serve as needed to hungry grillers and kids. Other guests will want to come closer to serving time. They too can have sausages, as well as the appetizers suggested in the menu. The point is, keep the guests fed and happy while they are waiting for the pork.

Grilling lots of cuts of meat of varying sizes is not an exact science, with precise formulas and timings. Your judgment and experience are invaluable, as is an instant-read thermometer. If you have ever grilled a large cut of meat, then you are familiar with the (usually male) ritual of gathering by the fire and debating whether something is done or not. Often this is punctuated by cutting into the meat a few times. While that is not fatal, it's much better to leave the meat intact, and that's where the thermometer comes in. Actually, I don't use one myself, but I have cooked so many cuts of meat in so many circumstances, I can tell by the touch if something is cooked: the meat has a certain feel or springiness.

The most important advice I can give you here is to be organized and to get as much done in advance as you can. A large meal with a lot of people inevitably raises the home cook's anxiety level. Clean the vegetables and prep them. Make your marinades and sauces (or at least partially make them). Think through all the utensils, cutting boards, serving forks, knives, etc., that you will need and have them at hand so that you are not running back and forth to the kitchen—or to the store to buy more charcoal. Remember, half the fun of a cookout is the social aspect. The more organized you are, the more you and your guests can enjoy yourselves.

Here are some things to include on your checklist for this grand *parrillada*: you'll need two grills, one for the pork, one for the vegetables. Ideally, you'll have a third spot where you can keep hardwood charcoal going to replenish the coals: say a smaller kettle grill or a chimney starter set on a rimmed fireproof base such as a terra-cotta flowerpot saucer. When it comes time to add more charcoal, lift the grate from the grill (with the aid of a helper) and add more hot charcoal. I recommend fireproof insulated barbecue gloves for handling the grate.

Use grilling trays or baskets to keep the herbs together as you grill them. Use kitchen twine to tie up the herb bundles. Bamboo skewers are useful for testing vegetables. You will need long-handled tongs, forks, and spatulas for turning; two large basting brushes; paper towels; and a cooler with ice and drinks. Have a bowl of water on hand to sprinkle on flare-ups.

Remember that when you are grilling, you can't walk away for very long. Have plenty of water to drink and wine to enjoy, but keep your eyes on the meats and veggies. Look at them with care and observe the transformations while you cook. It's the only way you will learn to be an expert.

Serving note: the meats will not all be at their perfect point of doneness at the same time. When a cut is done to taste, take it off the grill and carve some small pieces for your guests to enjoy standing around the grill with a glass of wine while they wait for the next one. Eventually, when all the meat is off the fire, you will sit down together for the feast.

SUGGESTED MENU FOR 18

Shaved Hearts of Celery with Portobello Mushrooms and Meyer Lemon (page 49)

Fig Salad with Burrata and Basil (page 30)

Pear Salad with Mint, Blue Cheese, and Fresh Dates (page 52)

Pork sausages

Various pork cuts with Charred Herb Salsa (page 122)

Grilled vegetables

Fresh fruit

Meats

The cuts may vary, depending on how your butcher breaks down a pig. The important thing is to get good-quality pork. The shoulder roasts and spareribs all need long, slow cooking to break down the collagen and become tender. Rib and loin chops cook more quickly, and shoulder chops and the sirloin roast are somewhere in between.

One 4½-pound bone-in pork shoulder roast
3 pounds spareribs (or more—they are always popular)
3 pounds country-style ribs
One 3-pound pork sirloin roast
4 pounds pork shoulder steaks
18 sweet pork sausages
5 pounds pork chops (bone-in)
Coarse salt
Freshly ground black pepper

Vegetables

The idea here is to buy whatever vegetables are in season and look good at the market. They are cooked until tender, cut in halves or quarters, seasoned with salt and pepper, and arranged on large platters with olive oil for drizzling. The list below is a typical selection.

6 beets, scrubbed
6 potatoes, scrubbed
6 sweet potatoes, scrubbed
2 large winter squash, such as butternut
6 onions
3 fennel bulbs, trimmed (reserve the fronds for the herb bundles)
4 red or yellow bell peppers
3 small to medium eggplants
Garlic bulbs
3 leeks, trimmed
8 tomatoes
4 zucchini
A bunch of kale, trimmed and tied together
A large head of bok choy, tied together with kitchen twine

SUGGESTED TIMELINE

ABOUT 1 WEEK AHEAD

■ Talk to your butcher about the meat and order it if necessary.

ONE OR MORE DAYS AHEAD

■ Check and clean your grills. Buy charcoal. Gather your tools. Grocery-shop.

DAY OF THE PARRILLADA

10:00 a.m. to Noon

■ Prepare the basting liquid.

Prepare two batches of this mixture, one for the pork and one for the vegetables. Keep each batch next to the appropriate grill to avoid cross-contamination.

2 lemons
2 cups dry white wine
2 cups extra virgin olive oil

Cut the lemons in half and squeeze the juice into a bowl. Add the white wine, olive oil, and squeezed lemon halves. Give it a stir to combine, and stir before each baste.

Noon

■ Start a charcoal fire in grill #1 for the pork.

12:30 p.m.

■ When you have a bed of mature coals, use a grill rake or hoe to arrange the coals in a 4-inch-wide strip around the perimeter of the grill.

■ Salt the large cuts of meat (shoulder roast, all the ribs, sirloin roast) all over and place bone side down in the center of the grill, not directly over the coals, so that they receive indirect heat. Sprinkle a little more salt on top.

1:00 p.m.

■ Turn the large cuts to expose an uncooked side to the heat and baste. (From now on, you will turn the meat every 30 minutes and baste it.)

1:30 p.m.

■ Start a charcoal fire in grill #2 for the vegetables. Turn the large cuts of meat and baste. Start a third batch of coals in your extra grill or chimney starter to use for replenishing as needed.

2:00 p.m.

■ Turn the large cuts again and baste. Place the shoulder steaks on the grill, over indirect heat.

■ Rake the coals in grill #2 so that they are evenly distributed and the fire will be at medium-low heat. Brush the grill grate with oil (use a scrunched-up paper towel held with tongs and dipped into a bowl of olive oil). Arrange the longer-cooking vegetables (beets, potatoes, sweet potatoes, winter squash, onions, and fennel) directly over the coals.

■ Replenish the coals in grill #1 as necessary to maintain medium-low heat.

2:30 p.m.

■ Turn the larger cuts of meat to another unexposed side, season with salt and pepper, and baste. Turn the shoulder steaks, season with salt and pepper, and baste.

■ Turn the larger vegetables. Timing for the vegetables will vary: Once they brown and soften on one side, they are ready to turn. They are done when you can stick a bamboo skewer or a sharp knife all the way through easily.

■ Arrange the softer vegetables (peppers, eggplants, garlic, leeks, tomatoes, zucchini, kale, and bok choy) on grill #2. As the vegetables soften and char, baste and turn them; pay close attention to the bok choy and kale, which will need plenty of basting. Put the herb bundles for the Charred Herb Salsa (page 122) on the grill and proceed as directed in the recipe.

3:00 p.m.

■ Replenish the coals in grill #2. (You will need someone to help you lift off the grate so you can distribute the fresh charcoal evenly.)

■ Replenish the coals around the outside of grill #1. Turn the large cuts of meat, season, and baste.

3:30 p.m.

■ Replenish the coals in both grills as necessary.

■ Place the smaller cuts of pork (chops, sausages) on grill #1. Turn the larger cuts and season and baste them. Check the internal temperatures of the large cuts; the sirloin roast should reach about 145°F for medium. Take it off when it's ready and let it rest.

■ Check the chops and sausages for doneness and turn as necessary, basting the chops.

■ Replenish the coals again as necessary. Arrange coal for three areas of varying heat: low, medium, and high.

4:00 p.m.

■ Continue to baste and check the vegetables, removing them to a platter as they are done.

■ Check the internal temperature of the large cuts again. The shoulder roast should be at 165° to 170°F when you remove it; carryover cooking will take it to 180°F as it rests. Remove a rack of ribs and cut into them to see if they are done. If not, return to the hottest side of the fire.

■ Move the chops so they are over hot coals to finish developing the crust if necessary. Finish the sausages over the hottest coals if necessary to develop a golden-brown crust.

4:30 p.m.

■ Reheat the vegetables over a medium fire if desired. Halve or quarter them before serving.

■ Meanwhile, serve the sausages.

■ Slice the chops and the sirloin roast and spoon some of the salsa over the slices.

■ Slice the racks of ribs into individual ribs. Dress with salsa as desired.

■ Carve the shoulder roast and dress with salsa. Serve all the meat.

■ Wine, wine, and more wine!

Charred Herb Salsa

This salsa is also great with Leg of Lamb (page 93) and Chicken on Strings (page 109). **MAKES ABOUT 4 CUPS**

FOR THE HERB BASTING LIQUID
2 lemons
2 cups dry white wine
2 cups extra virgin olive oil

FOR THE FIRST HERB BUNDLE
1 large bunch flat-leaf parsley
1 large bunch thyme
1 large bunch oregano
Reserved fennel fronds (from vegetables)
1 bunch scallions
3 garlic cloves

FOR THE SECOND HERB BUNDLE
1 bunch basil
1 bunch mint
1 bunch garlic scapes (you can also use young leeks, green garlic stalks, or garlic chives)

TO ASSEMBLE THE SALSA
1 bunch flat-leaf parsley, leaves removed and chopped
2 chile peppers (heat level to taste), seeded and minced, or more if desired
1 cup red wine vinegar, or to taste
1 cup extra virgin olive oil, or to taste
Coarse salt and freshly ground black pepper
Crushed red pepper flakes

For the basting liquid, remove the zest from the lemons in large strips and set aside. Cut the lemons in half and squeeze the juice into a large bowl. Add the white wine and olive oil and toss in the squeezed-out lemon halves.

For the first herb bundle, tie the parsley, thyme, oregano, fennel fronds, and scallions together with kitchen string. Tuck the strips of lemon zest and the garlic inside. For the second bundle, tie the basil, mint, and garlic scapes together.

One and a half hours before serving, put the herb bundles in grill baskets and set them on the grill with the vegetables. When they are slightly charred, remove the bundles and dunk them thoroughly in the basting liquid, then return them to the grill on the other side. Reserve the basting liquid for the salsa.

When the herbs are half charred on both sides, transfer them to a large chopping board. Trim off any tough stems and chop all the herbs together. Add the chopped fresh parsley and chile peppers and mix well, then stir it all into the remaining basting liquid. Add the vinegar and olive oil. Season with salt, pepper, and red pepper flakes to taste.

Braised Chorizo with Carrots, Fennel, and Creamy Polenta

Fresh chorizo sausage is a staple on the grill in Argentina and Uruguay, and it has recently become more widely available in the United States. Here I combine it with some spicy cured Spanish chorizo and lots of grated carrots and tomatoes to make a hearty stew, served over soft polenta. The carrots slowly cook down into the sauce to lighten it, and the sautéed fennel, incorporated at the end, adds texture.

SERVES 8 TO 12

FOR THE CHORIZO

¼ cup extra virgin olive oil, plus more for brushing

4 ounces thickly sliced pancetta, roughly chopped

1 onion, chopped

2 pounds fresh Argentine or Mexican-style chorizo, cut into 1-inch pieces

1½ pounds carrots, peeled and coarsely grated

8 ounces spicy (*picante*) cured Spanish chorizo, casings removed and diced

4 fresh rosemary sprigs

2 bay leaves

1 cup dry white wine

Two 28-ounce cans Italian plum tomatoes, with their juice

2 cups Rich Vegetable Stock (page 288)

2 fennel bulbs, trimmed, cored, and cut into julienne strips

Coarse salt and freshly ground black pepper

FOR THE POLENTA

8 cups Rich Vegetable Stock (page 288)

2 cups coarse polenta

¼ cup extra virgin olive oil

1 cup freshly grated Parmesan or Pecorino Romano cheese

Coarse salt and freshly ground black pepper

To make the chorizo, heat 2 tablespoons of the olive oil in a deep heavy pot over medium heat. Add the pancetta and sauté for several minutes, until the fat starts to render, then add the onions, stirring to coat them in the fat. When the onions have softened, add the fresh chorizo, stir well, and cook, stirring, until it loses its raw color. Add the carrots, Spanish chorizo, and herbs and stir well. Cover the pot and let the carrots sweat for several minutes to soften them.

Uncover the pot and add the wine. Raise the heat, bring to a boil, and let the mixture bubble until the wine reduces by half. Stir in the tomatoes, with their juice, and the stock. Crush the tomatoes with the back of a fork, then lower the heat to a bare simmer, partially cover, and cook for 4 hours. The carrots will melt into the sauce with the tomatoes. (The recipe can be prepared ahead to this point; reheat before adding the fennel.)

About 20 minutes before serving, prepare the polenta: Bring the stock to a boil in a large heavy saucepan. Gradually stir in the polenta and let it bubble over medium heat, stirring frequently, for 15 to 20 minutes, until it is thick and creamy but still quite moist. Beat in the olive oil and cheese and season to taste with salt and pepper.

Meanwhile, toss the fennel with the remaining 2 tablespoons olive oil in a bowl. Heat a *chapa* or a large cast-iron griddle over medium-low heat and brush with olive oil. When the oil is hot, add the fennel and sauté gently, turning occasionally, for about 8 minutes, until crisp and golden on all sides. Stir into the stew and season with salt and pepper to taste.

Spoon the polenta into large bowls, top with the braised chorizo, and serve.

ABOVE: The old abandoned train station in Garzón. **OPPOSITE:** Pork Chops with Toasted Nuts (page 128) and Braised Beans with Red Wine and Tomato (page 215).

Pork Chops
with Toasted Nuts

The very best pork comes from free-range pigs that eat grass and nuts, particularly acorns, so I thought nicely caramelized pork would be wonderful with toasted nuts: the two would accentuate each other. Use big, thick pork chops for this, such as the large porterhouse chops available at some farmers' markets or at specialty butchers. They are well suited to the heat of a *chapa,* where they develop a beautiful crust and moist, juicy interior. **SERVES 4**

¼ cup oregano oil (see page 281),
    at room temperature
4 pork chops (bone-in), about ¾ inch thick
    (14 ounces each)
Coarse salt and freshly ground black pepper
Braised Beans with Red Wine and Tomato
    (page 215)
¼ cup chopped Toasted Nuts (page 283)
Celery leaves (optional)

Spread the oregano oil on a large plate and turn the chops in it to coat. Season well with salt and pepper and let marinate for at least 30 minutes.

Heat the grill or one or two large, ridged, cast-iron grill pans over medium heat. Season the chops well with salt, arrange them on the hot surface, and cook for 6 to 8 minutes, until nicely grill-marked on the bottom. Turn and cook the other side for 4 to 6 minutes, or until the meat reaches an internal temperature of 140°F; it should be slightly pink inside. Transfer to a platter and let rest for 5 minutes.

Meanwhile, bring the beans to a simmer. Check and adjust the seasoning if necessary.

Spoon the beans into wide soup bowls and arrange the chops on top. Top with the toasted nuts and garnish with celery leaves, if using.

PICTURED ON PAGE 127

Grilled and Roasted Leg of Pork Wrapped in Rosemary with Orange, Black Pepper, and Rosemary Salmuera

This is a dramatic dish for a family gathering or a holiday party. Inevitably, there will be leftovers—that's a good thing—just as with a Thanksgiving turkey. You'll also have a flavorful bone to cook with beans. Serve with the salmuera or Roasted Pineapple (page 254).

If you have room in your fridge, wrap the roast in the rosemary and garlic the night before for deeper flavor. If you can start the pork on the grill outside, you get the benefit of smoky wood flavor, but it will still be delicious if you do all the cooking in the oven.

And, if you love this idea but don't want to roast a whole leg, try it with a half leg and adjust the timing accordingly. **SERVES ABOUT 20, WITH LEFTOVERS**

1 pork leg (on the bone), about 22 pounds, with about ¾ inch fat left on
Coarse salt
3 or more bunches rosemary
12 garlic cloves, cut in half
Orange, Black Pepper, and Rosemary Salmuera (page 287)

Set the meat on a large work surface and, using a sharp knife, make deep lengthwise cuts in the fat from one end of the leg to the other, forming grooves about 1½ inches apart—do not cut into the meat, just through the fat. Repeat with crosswise cuts the same distance apart to form a crosshatch pattern. Sprinkle generously all over with salt and rub it thoroughly into the fat and meat. Turn the leg fat side up and, starting at one end, line the grooves with rosemary branches, pressing in as much rosemary as you can. Slide a piece of butcher's twine under the center of the leg, bring both ends up, and tie it tightly to hold the rosemary in place. Repeat with a second length of twine a few inches away from the first, and a third a few inches away on the other side. Repeat with more twine until the rosemary is firmly secured. Tuck the garlic cloves into the crosswise cuts, under the rosemary or twine if necessary to hold it in. Wrap in foil and refrigerate, overnight if possible. Bring to room temperature before roasting.

If starting the roast outdoors, prepare a medium-low fire in a charcoal grill and heat an *horno* or the oven to 325°F, with the rack set low enough to leave at least 2 inches of space above the top of the roast. If cooking only indoors, heat the *horno* or oven to 425°F.

If cooking outdoors, place the meat on the fire and grill slowly, turning it to brown the fat on all sides. Then transfer it to a roasting pan, cover with a double thickness of foil, and place in the *horno* or oven. If working only indoors, put the meat in a large deep roasting pan or turkey roaster and brown it in the hot oven for 25 minutes, or until the fat starts to crisp and the rosemary is very fragrant. Remove the roasting pan from the oven and cover tightly with a double layer of foil, then return it to the oven and reduce the heat to 325°F. In either case, cook, covered, for 4 hours.

Uncover the meat and spoon or pour off most of the fat. Raise the heat to 350°F, baste the meat with some of the fat, and return it to the oven for another 2 hours, or until a digital-probe or instant-read thermometer stuck in the thickest part registers 150°F and the fat is crisp and brown. During this time, check the meat occasionally and spoon off the fat if necessary; if the roast is browning too quickly, cover it loosely with foil. Transfer the meat to a large carving board, cover it loosely with foil, and let it rest for 30 minutes. The internal temperature will continue to rise as it rests.

To carve, cut thin slices inward toward the bone, then cut across them at the bone to release them. Reserve all the juices on the carving board to spoon over the meat. Arrange on plates, spoon the juices over, and serve with the salmuera.

PICTURED ON PAGES 130–131

Grilled and Roasted Leg of Pork Wrapped in Rosemary with
Orange, Black Pepper, and Rosemary Salmuera (page 129).

Red-Wine-Braised Spareribs with Red Cabbage and Carrot Slaw

In the United States, people are very fond of spareribs either grilled or smoked, but they are very nice when braised too. The richer and more flavorful the braising liquid, the more delicious the result. So go ahead and enjoy your barbecued ribs all summer long, but when winter comes, this is just the thing. When possible, I grill the ribs first for more flavor, but you can also brown them in a pot on the stovetop. Instead of braising the ribs with red cabbage—which invariably results in overdone cabbage—I serve my cabbage as a crunchy bright slaw. SERVES 6

6 pounds spareribs or country-style ribs
Coarse salt and freshly ground black pepper
1 bottle (750 ml) full-bodied red wine, such as
    Malbec, plus more if needed
3 cups Rich Brown Pork Stock (page 289), plus
    more if needed
2 heads garlic, halved horizontally
3 bay leaves
6 fresh thyme sprigs
4 fresh rosemary sprigs
Red Cabbage and Carrot Slaw (page 223)

If starting the ribs outdoors, prepare a medium fire in a charcoal grill. Trim the excess fat from the ribs and season them well with salt and pepper. Grill the ribs, turning often, for about 30 minutes, until crisp and brown on both sides. (Alternatively, working in batches to avoid crowding, season the ribs, lay them fat side down in a large heavy pot, and slowly brown them over medium heat, turning them as they darken and crisp on both sides. Spoon or pour off the fat.)

Meanwhile, heat an *horno* or the oven to 350°F.

Transfer the grilled ribs to a large heavy pot. Pour the wine over the ribs and add enough stock to almost cover them. Add the garlic and herbs and season with salt and pepper. Bring to a boil, then set in the oven and braise for about 2½ hours, or until the meat is tender enough to cut with a spoon. Every half hour or so, skim off the fat, turn the meat, and add more stock or wine if necessary. Eventually the liquid should reduce to a deep, burnished-mahogany syrup.

When the ribs are done, transfer them to a large deep serving platter or a bowl and cover with foil. Strain the sauce through a fine-mesh strainer into a bowl and skim as much fat as you can off the top. (At this point, the sauce can be chilled, which will make it easier to remove the fat, and the ribs refrigerated, to serve the next day; reheat the ribs in the sauce before serving.) Adjust the seasoning.

To serve, spoon a generous amount of sauce over the ribs to moisten and glaze them. Serve with the cabbage slaw and the rest of the sauce on the side.

Pork Loin Chops with Thyme Oil and Roasted Grapes on the Vine

Few things are more rewarding than a succulent pork chop, and few things are more disappointing than one that is dried out. Grilled pork chops require care. Thyme oil infuses the chops with an herb that I find particularly beautiful with pork—it builds flavor but doesn't take over the way rosemary might. As for the roasted grapes, everyone loves wine with pork, and wine is made from grapes, so I thought, "Why not?"
SERVES 4

4 boneless pork loin chops, about ¾ inch thick and
    8 ounces each
3 tablespoons thyme oil (see page 281), at room
    temperature
Coarse salt and freshly ground black pepper
8 small fresh thyme sprigs
1 tablespoon extra virgin olive oil
Roasted Grapes on the Vine (page 282)

Pat the pork chops dry with paper towels and put them on a plate. Spoon a little thyme oil on each one and turn them over in it to coat both sides. Season well with salt and pepper and top each chop with a couple of sprigs of thyme, pressing on them so they adhere.

Heat a charcoal grill or a large deep-ridged cast-iron grill pan over high heat. Brush the grill or pan with oil. Add the pork chops, thyme side down, and grill for about 4 minutes, or until nicely marked on the bottom. Turn and grill on the other side for about 3 minutes, or until browned but still just slightly pink inside.

Arrange the chops on dinner plates, with a bunch of roasted grapes on top of each one, and serve immediately.

PICTURED ON PAGE 137

TRAVELS WITH FIRE

NEW YORK,
NEW YORK

Cooking in front of Gramercy Tavern in Manhattan.

New York can be generous, warm, and loving when the mood strikes, but it can turn capricious, unforgiving, and frantic just as easily. I have seen both sides. I spent five years in the Hamptons, and I tried very hard to open a place in New York City. So expensive! And so many rules— especially for a man who wants to cook over open fire. I think in the years I was there it was probably easier to get a permit to use dynamite than one to cook over a wood fire.

But then there is the other New York, the Big Apple, the city with the strongest pulse of any place in the world. So many nationalities! And all of them cook. On a recent trip, I was invited by the charity organization Share Our Strength to cook on the street in front of the famous Gramercy Tavern. It was quite a sight, with our *infiernillos* blazing, taxi drivers passing and waving, and passengers in long black limousines rolling down their windows to breathe in the smell of fire and beef. A policeman stopped, and

I was worried that with all the smoke and flames he would shut us down. I told him that we were just about done and would have the fires out right away.

"Hey," he said, "keep them going. I want a taste. It looks so good." A classic streetwise New York cop! Right out of the movies.

And then there's Brooklyn. It might be the most exciting place in the food world right now: people making the best chocolate I've ever tasted. Farmers and beekeepers working on the rooftops of old factories. Young chefs creating pure flavors and mixing different ethnic foods with no regard to any rules other than that it must taste good and be interesting. We cooked under the Brooklyn Bridge as the rising sun lit up the skyline of Wall Street. We took our grills to the streets of the gritty old neighborhood of Bushwick. It looked so forbidding, reminding me of how people told me the Buenos Aires neighborhood of La Boca was too rough for a fine restaurant when I moved there years ago. But Bushwick, like La Boca, was alive with youth and the excitement of urban pioneers.

One morning I took my grill to Red Hook, an ancient waterfront neighborhood. This was shortly before the greatest storm in the city's history would wash away the very ground we had stood on and invade the streets like a marauding army. But on that peaceful late summer day, the breeze blew off the harbor; flights of ducks and geese, a mile long, made their way south for the winter; and feeding seagulls created mayhem as they dove into schools of baitfish that were penned up by hordes of migrating striped bass. A riot of nature in the midst of this stylish, sophisticated city, within sight of the skyscrapers where hedge-fund billionaires were involved in a different kind of feeding frenzy.

BIRDS

Smashed Chicken Breast in a Tomato Crust with Tomato and
Arugula Salad (page 148).

Smashed Chicken Breast in a Potato Crust with Tomato and Arugula Salad

Because chicken breasts are relatively thick, by the time the inside cooks through, the outside can be tough and lifeless. By pounding the breasts, you can cook the chicken rapidly so that it remains tender and juicy inside its "overcoat" of crisp potato slices. Here you need to monitor the heat so that the potatoes brown and crust over slowly. The result is two kinds of crunchiness, from the seared chicken and the potato crust. When I serve a *milanesa* (breaded veal chop), I like a fresh garden salad of ripe tomatoes, sharp onions, and greens, so I figured, "If it's good for the calf, it's good for the chicken."

Use the removable bottom of a 9-inch tart pan to flip the chicken. The round shape makes it easier to slide it under the potatoes in a circular scooping motion, which helps the potatoes stick together and remain on the chicken. (If you don't have one, use one or two wide spatulas.) **SERVES 2**

**1 whole boneless chicken breast, skin on, about
    1 pound**
Coarse salt and freshly ground black pepper
½ teaspoon crushed red pepper flakes, or to taste
2 Idaho (baking) potatoes, scrubbed
**About 2 tablespoons extra virgin olive oil, plus
    more for drizzling**
**About 6 tablespoons unsalted butter, cut into small
    pieces**
1 large ripe tomato, cut into bite-sized pieces
½ small red onion, sliced very thin
1 small bunch arugula, tough stems removed

Lay the chicken skin side down on a work surface and pound it with a mallet to a thickness of about ¾ inch. Trim off any ragged edges. Season generously with salt, black pepper, and the red pepper flakes.

Slice the potatoes paper-thin on a mandoline. (Do not rinse or wipe them—you want to retain the starch.) Arrange an overlapping circle of potato slices around the top edge of the chicken, extending about ⅓ inch over the edge. Working toward the center, continue until you have a spiraling layer of potato slices covering the entire surface of the chicken. Press down firmly on the potatoes with the palm of your hand to set them in place.

Heat a *chapa* or a large cast-iron griddle over medium heat. Brush the hot surface generously with olive oil and dot it with half the butter. When the butter melts and begins to foam, slide the bottom of a metal tart pan beneath the chicken to lift it and invert it, potato side down, onto the hot *chapa*. Tuck any stray potato slices back in, and cook, undisturbed, for about 12 minutes; watch the edges of the potatoes from the side as they soften, curl, and start to release from the hot surface, becoming crisp and brown on the bottom. Lower the heat if necessary to prevent burning, and add more butter or oil to the *chapa* as it is absorbed by the potatoes.

When a bamboo skewer pierces the potatoes easily, they are cooked through. Season the chicken skin with salt and pepper, then carefully slide the metal disk underneath the potatoes in the same direction as the spiral, using a deliberate, circular scooping motion to keep the potatoes in line, and flip the chicken over. Cook for about 8 minutes more, blotting up excess fat with a paper towel as necessary, or adding dots of butter or oil if the griddle seems dry. When the chicken is cooked through but still juicy, slide the disk under it again and transfer it to a platter.

Meanwhile, toss the tomato, onion, and arugula together in a bowl with a light drizzle of olive oil. Arrange the salad on top of the chicken, and serve cut into wedges like a pizza.

PICTURED ON PAGES 144 AND 146–147

Butterflied Chicken a la Parrilla with Chanterelles and Grilled Chicory

A grilled split chicken, golden brown as it comes from the *parrilla,* is one of my favorite dishes. Salt and pepper are all it needs. Such a simple preparation wants an equally uncomplicated but flavorful side dish. Chicory, which I learned to love when I worked in Italy as a young man, does the trick for me every time. Brushed with olive oil, seasoned with salt and pepper, and grilled to crispness, it is as good as the chicken that it graces. If you are lucky enough to have acquired some chanterelles or other wild mushrooms to sauté, they make the crowning touch. Their color is like the caramelized crust of the chicken.

I butterfly my chickens differently than most butchers: I split them through the breastbone instead of the back, leaving the backbone in instead of discarding it. I think you get a juicier chicken this way, and an extra fun bone to pick. **SERVES 4**

1 farm-raised chicken, about 3 pounds
Coarse salt and freshly ground black pepper
Extra virgin olive oil

FOR THE CHANTERELLES
4 tablespoons unsalted butter
2 tablespoons extra virgin olive oil
1 large shallot, finely chopped
1 large garlic clove, minced
1 pound chanterelles or other mushrooms,
    cleaned, trimmed, and left whole if small,
    cut in half or into thirds if larger
¼ cup chopped fresh flat-leaf parsley

1 large bunch young chicory or frisée, cut in half
Extra virgin olive oil for drizzling

With kitchen shears, split the chicken through the breastbone and press it out flat. Pat it dry on both sides with paper towels. Sprinkle with salt and pepper.

Heat a charcoal grill or a large deep-ridged cast-iron grill pan over medium heat. Brush the grate or ridges generously with oil. When the oil starts to smoke, add the chicken bone side down and grill until it browns and crisps on the first side, about 15 minutes. Turn the chicken and grill on the other side for 10 to 15 minutes more, until it is cooked through. Transfer to a platter and let it rest.

Meanwhile, for the mushrooms, heat half the butter and half the olive oil in a large skillet over medium-low heat. Add the shallots and sauté over medium heat for several minutes, stirring occasionally, until they soften. Add the garlic and sauté until the shallots are translucent, adjusting the heat as necessary so the garlic does not burn. Add the mushrooms and the remaining butter and oil and sauté for about 8 minutes, until the mushrooms have released their liquid and it has reduced with the butter into a light glaze. Stir in the parsley and keep warm.

While the chicken rests, drizzle the chicory with a little oil, place it on the hottest part of the grill, or in the blotted grill pan over high heat, and cook for a few minutes, turning once, until lightly charred. Cut the chicory into serving pieces.

Cut the chicken into serving pieces and serve with the mushrooms and chicory.

PICTURED ON PAGES 150–151

OPPOSITE AND ABOVE: Butterflied Chicken a la Parrilla with
Chanterelles and Grilled Chicory (page 149).

In the Snow

Snow is a language I understand. I think in Spanish. I babble in English. I munch French. I sing Portuguese. I make my way around some German poems. I speak Snow.

Whenever I see a snowstorm rumbling down from the Andes toward my home on The Island, I am transported back to childhood. I can't sit still. I press my face up against the windowpane and watch the clouds roll in. I check the thermometer and then glance back at the mountains. I watch the birds doing whatever it is they do to make ready for snow. They seem so busy! I step outside to smell the air and then I duck back into the warmth of the cabin. I will go on like this—restless with anticipation—for hours. I think it must be unbearable to be around me at such times, I am so full of nervous energy.

But then, when the blizzard starts and I feel we are going to get at least six feet of snow (no kidding), I relax. Maybe I'll read for a while, or bake a chocolate cake, which is one of the special things that I do only at The Island. Inevitably, my thoughts will turn to my next cookout in the snow. It is both a challenge and a pleasure.

I load up a sleigh with dry wood, pots and pans, food and wine, and a duffel bag and warm blankets for the dog and then I head for a cooking site—usually beside a stream whose water still runs silvery clear in the winter. I pick a fire site and tamp down the snow all around so that it is firm enough to walk on, then lay a piece of sheet metal—say 3 feet by 3 feet—on the snow. I will build my fire on the metal (if I didn't do that, the fire would melt the snow underneath and the water would put the fire out before I got a chance to cook). If the snow isn't deep, no metal needed: I just clear away the snow until I see ground.

Time to start the fire and open a bottle of wine. The meal will usually begin with a hearty soup that I make in a cast-iron cauldron, suspended from some stakes—lots of onions and garlic to ward off the cold, and some creamy sweet butternut squash to warm your insides. Meanwhile I'll roast whatever meat I've brought, very slowly, perhaps impaling it on a sapling stuck into the snow. The vegetables are easy: some potatoes and fennel thrown into the ashes and embers. For dessert, burnt apples and oranges with rosemary and honey.

So simple!

Then, when we have eaten and drunk our fill, it is nice to lie back to watch the stars, to listen to the wolves, and—if you have chosen well—to cuddle with your guest.

Griddled Chicken
with Charred Herb and Tomato Salad

The chicken cooks very slowly, and at first it may look as if it won't cook through. But don't worry: the skin becomes crisp as the fat renders, and the result is very succulent meat. I serve it with a colorful salad. The combination of basil and mint keeps things light and fresh tasting. The char on the herbs should be very subtle—you don't want them to lose their freshness and flavorful but volatile oils. If the chicken breasts are large, cut them in half and put them on the griddle after the legs and thighs have cooked for a few minutes; the smaller pieces will crisp up and stay juicier. Don't crowd the griddle: here as elsewhere, only real generosity of space allows food to cook, crust, and char. **SERVES 4**

**One 3-pound chicken, cut into serving pieces
   (breasts, drumsticks, and thighs)**
Sea salt and freshly ground black pepper
3 tablespoons extra virgin olive oil
1 pound assorted small heirloom tomatoes
12 large fresh basil leaves
12 large fresh mint leaves
6 fresh thyme sprigs
2 fresh rosemary sprigs
1 large garlic clove, minced
1 small red onion, sliced very thin

Pat the chicken pieces very dry with paper towels. If the breasts are large, cut them in half. Season with salt and pepper.

Heat a *chapa* or a large cast-iron griddle over medium heat. Brush the surface with 2 teaspoons of the olive oil. When it begins to shimmer, add the chicken pieces, skin side down. As the chicken pieces brown, turn them to cook on all sides; it will take about 30 minutes for legs and thighs, less for cut-up breasts. As the smaller pieces are done, take them off the grill while the others continue cooking.

Meanwhile, cut the tomatoes in half, or in quarters if they are on the larger side. Place the herbs in a bowl with the minced garlic, the remaining olive oil, the onion, and tomatoes. Season to taste with salt and pepper.

After the chicken has cooked for about 20 minutes, add the tomatoes and herbs to the *chapa* and cook the tomatoes on one side until lightly charred.

Arrange the chicken and the warm herb and tomato salad on a large platter, season the chicken with salt and a few grinds of pepper, and serve immediately.

Duck Breast
with Balsamic Vinegar and Asparagus

Duck breasts, rich and fatty, are well suited to the *chapa*. Low, even heat and slow cooking melts the fat away, crisps the skin, and brings the meat to a perfect medium-rare. It has some of the intensity of wild game but a softer texture, like that of strip steak. Real balsamic vinegar has both the subtlety and the strength to stand up to the duck. By real balsamic vinegar, I mean the aged and concentrated vinegar made in Modena, not the sugar-sweetened vinegar you find in the supermarket, which is an abomination.

Using a skillet instead of a griddle makes it easier to spoon off the fat as the duck cooks. **SERVES 4**

**2 magrets (Moulard duck breasts), about 1 pound
  each**
Coarse salt and freshly ground black pepper
**2 large Idaho (baking) potatoes, peeled and cut
  lengthwise into quarters**
2 tablespoons extra virgin olive oil
4 tablespoons unsalted butter, cut into small pieces
1 red onion, thinly sliced
1 pound thin asparagus, trimmed and cut in half
1½ cups aged balsamic vinegar

Pat the duck breasts dry with paper towels. Using a small sharp knife, score the fat in a crosshatch pattern, with about ⅓ inch between cuts. This will allow the fat to melt and render easily. Season with salt and pepper.

Heat a large cast-iron skillet over medium heat. Place the magrets skin side down on the hot surface and cook for about 15 minutes, carefully spooning off the fat as it melts, so the skin crisps, and reserving it in a bowl. Lower the heat if the skin appears to be browning before the fat renders—it is worth the extra few minutes for a crisp end result. When the skin is crisp and golden, turn the breasts

to the other side and cook for another 5 minutes or so, until the meat is medium-rare when you cut into it with a knife. Transfer to a carving board and let rest while you prepare the vegetables and sauce.

Slice the quartered potatoes very thin on a mandoline. (Do not wipe them off—you want to retain the starch.) Brush a large cast-iron griddle with the olive oil and heat over medium heat. Dot with half the butter, and when it foams, spread the potatoes and onions out on the hot surface. Cook, without moving them, for several minutes, until the potatoes soften and stick together and the onions start to brown nicely on the bottom; add more butter as it is absorbed and drizzle with a tablespoon or so of the rendered duck fat. With a wide sharp-edged spatula, turn the vegetables over to cook on the other side. Arrange the asparagus around the vegetables, dot with the remaining butter, and drizzle with a tablespoon or so of the duck fat; turn the asparagus as it softens and browns. Remove the vegetables to a serving platter as they are done and season to taste with salt and pepper.

Meanwhile, to prepare the sauce, remove as much fat from the skillet as you can, leaving the caramelized duck juices. Turn the heat to medium-high and, averting your face, carefully pour the vinegar into the skillet, scraping up the bits on the bottom with a spatula. Continue to cook until the vinegar reduces to a rich syrup. Return the magrets to the pan and turn them in the hot syrup for a moment, then remove the skillet from the heat, transfer the magrets back to the carving board, and slice them across the grain.

Arrange the duck on the platter with the vegetables, spoon the remaining glaze over the duck, and serve immediately.

When I first came to Uruguay, if you headed east and north along the coast road from the tourist mecca of Punta del Este, you would have found a long row of ghost towns, or no towns at all.

To reach my little restaurant, which sat on the beach in the shadow of the lighthouse of José Ignacio, you had to take a ferry across the lagoon. It was splendidly isolated. But with the coming of the roads, development followed, and that isolation departed. In those early years, I would go to Garzón, a little town about fifteen minutes inland. It was indeed a bit of a ghost town itself, with very few people and many empty houses from the colonial era. The mayor of José Ignacio lived there, so I would often visit to take care of business matters. Or I would stop off after going into the hills to buy some stone for my endless construction projects at the restaurant.

Though Garzón was humbled by the passage of time, I thought it had very fine "bones": a pretty little plaza, wide streets encircling it, old houses, two old churches, and beautiful palmera trees with their sprays of orange berries. And then there were the people. The more I visited, the more I admired their quiet and polite ways.

Ten years ago, I bought the old general store and began to convert it into a restaurant and hotel. People liked it so much that they began to buy neighboring properties and renovate them. The pace of life quickened just a little. "Rush hour" still means a moped, car, or horse going by every ten minutes or so. The town philosophers still gather at the beer hall a block from the town square, and at night, you can still hear the sound of the children's swing set creaking in the wind that blows across the plaza.

Much as I love this little village, once it started to develop, I sought out the solitude that had drawn me there in the first place. I bought a property ten minutes farther on in the green hills, which, viewed from on high, seem to roll on forever in rippling undulations of deep green. People don't think of Uruguay as having dramatic scenery, and it doesn't have the looming mountains and ice-blue glaciers of Patagonia, but when you build a bonfire on a hilltop and roast some meat and look out at the countryside as the sun sets, you will never find a more thrilling view.

I am at peace in Garzón.

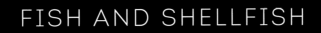

FISH AND SHELLFISH

Churrasco of Tuna with Coal-Burnt Pimentón Oil, Heirloom Tomato and Chard Salad, and Garlicky Potato Puree

Churrasco is usually a quickly cooked beefsteak, but the technique is well suited to tuna, which is best seared well on the outside and still almost raw within. Yellowfin tuna works beautifully here. I never use the endangered bluefin, and I encourage you to avoid it.

I serve the tuna with a warm salad of chard stems flavored with a smoky pimentón and garlic olive oil, which has been graced by a burning ember from the fire. This is very smoky and is best made outdoors; indoors, you can make a quick infused oil with smoked pimentón. Chard stems have the consistency of celery stalks but some acidity and tang, which goes nicely with a fatty fish like tuna, likewise the sweet and tangy tomato. The olives stand in contrast to all the milder tasting vegetables and creamy potatoes.

It's important that the griddle be very hot so the tuna doesn't stick. **SERVES 4**

2 tablespoons Coal-Burnt Pimentón Oil (recipe follows)
or
1 teaspoon smoked pimentón de La Vera, plus more if desired
2 tablespoons extra virgin olive oil
1 garlic clove, minced

FOR THE POTATO PUREE
1 garlic clove, minced
¼ cup extra virgin olive oil
1½ pounds Idaho (baking) potatoes, peeled
½ cup milk, plus more if necessary
Coarse salt and freshly ground black pepper
Tiny pinch of freshly grated nutmeg

FOR THE SALAD
1 pound small red, yellow, and green heirloom tomatoes, quartered
Stems from 1 bunch rainbow chard (leaves reserved for another use)
1 tablespoon extra virgin olive oil, plus more for brushing

½ cup mild Greek olives, smashed and pitted
Fleur de sel
Freshly ground black pepper

1 pound ¾-inch-thick fresh tuna steaks, cut into 8 pieces

If you do not have the coal-burnt oil, put the smoked pimentón in a small bowl and whisk in the olive oil and minced garlic. Let infuse for at least 15 minutes; strain the garlic out of the oil before using.

To prepare the potato puree, combine the minced garlic with the olive oil in a small bowl and set aside to infuse while you boil the potatoes. Cut the potatoes into 2-inch pieces, put them in a saucepan with water to cover by about 2 inches, and bring to a boil over medium-high heat. Reduce the heat and simmer for 15 minutes, or until the potatoes are soft enough to mash with a fork. Drain the potatoes in a colander and pass through a food mill back into the hot saucepan (off the heat) to dry out for a minute or two.

Strain the garlic from the olive oil and add it to the ½ cup milk in a small saucepan. Bring just to a boil (watching carefully so it doesn't boil over), then remove from the heat and beat into the mashed potatoes. Season carefully with salt, pepper, and the nutmeg. Keep warm until serving time by setting the saucepan over a larger pot of simmering water; beat in a little more hot milk just before serving, if it seems dry.

Heat a *chapa* or a large cast-iron griddle over high heat. Toss the tomatoes and chard stems with 1 tablespoon of olive oil. Brush the hot surface with plain olive oil, and when it shimmers, add the tomatoes and chard stems. Cook, without disturbing them, for about 3 minutes, until nicely browned on the bottom. Turn the vegetables, add the smashed olives, and cook for another minute or two, until the chard is tender. Transfer the tomatoes, chard, and olives to a bowl and toss gently with

1 tablespoon of the pimentón oil. Season to taste with fleur de sel and pepper. Set aside.

Brush the tuna steaks with some of the pimentón oil. Wipe off the *chapa* and brush with olive oil. When it shimmers, add the tuna steaks, spaced well apart, and cook on the first side for just a minute or two, until browned on the bottom. Brush with pimentón oil, turn the tuna, and cook very briefly on the other side, less than a minute. The tuna should still be rare inside. Brush with the remaining pimentón oil and sprinkle with fleur de sel and a bit more pimentón, if desired.

Spread a swath of hot potato puree on each of four dinner plates. Set the tuna beside the potatoes, along with the tomato chard salad.

PICTURED ON PAGE 172

Coal-Burnt Pimentón Oil

Because this is very smoky, it should be made outdoors. A live ember from the fire is submerged into olive oil, which immediately extinguishes it, while the coal flavors the oil. The oil must be at room temperature or cooler—hot oil will catch fire.
MAKES 2 CUPS

2 cups extra virgin olive oil
¼ cup pimentón dulce (sweet Spanish paprika)
1 teaspoon minced garlic (optional)

Have a metal bowl of water handy. If you have long hair, make sure it is tied back.

Pour the olive oil into a deep metal bowl and stir in the pimentón. Using a pair of tongs, pick up a small glowing ember from a grill fire and, holding onto the tongs and averting your face, carefully plunge it deep into the oil; the oil should extinguish the flame. Remove the ember and transfer it to the bowl of water to make sure it is completely extinguished (and take care to discard it safely).

Add the optional minced garlic and set aside for 30 minutes. Strain before using. The oil can be refrigerated for several days.

OPPOSITE: Churrasco of Tuna with Coal-Burnt Pimentón Oil (page 170).

Skate a la Plancha with Braised White Beans, Garlic, and Parsley

In Paris, skate with brown butter and capers is a bistro classic, but back in Patagonia, when I beheld a very pretty fresh-caught skate, just pulled from the cold waters of the South Atlantic, I thought it needed no more fussing than some oil and seasoning and a few moments on my *chapa*. Creamy white beans with aromatic vegetables make for a smooth and flavorful side dish that complements the texture of properly cooked skate. **SERVES 4**

About 2 cups (12 ounces) dried cannellini or other small white beans, picked over and soaked overnight in water to cover
8 cups Rich Vegetable Stock (page 288)
6 tablespoons extra virgin olive oil, plus more for drizzling
2 spring onions or 6 scallions, chopped (about 1 cup)
2 leeks, white and pale green parts only, chopped
1 red chile pepper, seeded and finely chopped
1 large red bell pepper, cored, seeded, and chopped
6 garlic cloves, chopped
Coarse salt and freshly ground black pepper
4 boneless skate wings, about 6 ounces each
1½ cups chopped fresh flat-leaf parsley

Drain the beans and rinse, then put them in a large heavy pot, cover with the vegetable stock, and bring to a boil over medium heat. Skim off any foam, reduce the heat to a low simmer, and cook the beans gently for 30 to 45 minutes, until they are almost tender. (Timing will depend on the freshness of the beans.) Drain, reserving the broth.

Heat 3 tablespoons of the olive oil in a heavy casserole over medium-low heat. Add the onions, leeks, chile pepper, bell pepper, and one-third of the chopped garlic and cook until the vegetables are softened but not browned. Add the beans with 2 cups of the reserved broth, giving them a gentle stir to combine without breaking them. Taste and season with salt and pepper, keeping in mind that the seasoning will be concentrated as the liquid

reduces. Cook very gently for about 20 minutes, until the beans are tender, the liquid is absorbed by the beans, and the flavors are blended; if the liquid evaporates before the beans are cooked, add more as needed. Adjust the seasoning and set aside.

Meanwhile, pat the skate wings dry. Season both sides with salt and pepper. Drizzle half the remaining olive oil over a large plate or tray and scatter ¾ cup of the parsley and half the remaining chopped garlic over it. Lay the skate wings in one layer on top. Scatter ½ cup of the parsley leaves and the remaining chopped garlic over the skate, drizzle the rest of the olive oil over the top, and turn the skate a couple of times to coat. Set aside for 20 minutes.

Heat a *chapa* or a large cast-iron griddle over medium-high heat. Brush the hot surface with olive oil and set the skate wings on it. Cook the fish, without moving it, for about 3 minutes, until the bottom is nicely browned. Using a wide, sharp spatula, carefully turn the fish to cook on the other side. After a minute or so, when the ribs of the wings begin to separate, the fish is done.

Transfer the skate to serving plates and spoon the beans alongside. Sprinkle with the remaining ¼ cup parsley, drizzle with olive oil, and serve.

NOTES: When Brazilians serve beans, they often start the meal by drinking a glass of the bean juice with a chaser of cachaça (a potent liquor made from distilled sugarcane juice), muddled with hot chiles. It's a real eye-opener.

Buy beans from purveyors who have good turnover and can be relied on for fresh batches. The older the beans, the longer they will take to cook.

Cannellini beans have a thin skin and should be simmered very gently so they get creamy inside but don't break up. The beans can be cooked well in advance. You can make a great soup with the leftover broth garnished with croutons brushed with rosemary oil. The beans can also be pureed for a side dish, or mashed on rosemary–olive oil crostini for an appetizer or party snack.

Grilled Whole Fish Stuffed with Fennel

I love grilling whole fish after slashing the sides and stuffing the slashes with flavorful herbs, vegetables, ham, or anything else that adds contrasting flavor and texture. I adore the undisciplined look of fish done this way as it sits on the grill. Here the fennel, with its light hint of licorice, complements the fish without dominating it. The fennel within the fish steams while the outside chars for contrast: two tastes from the same ingredient. Any torpedo-shaped fish, such as snapper, small bluefish, weakfish, or sea trout, works well with this technique, though you will have to play with the grill timing according to the size of the fish.

I had never grilled dressed greens until I created these for Alice Waters, when I cooked with my fires at Chez Panisse. I was inspired by the beauty of the fresh kale, and I wanted to grill it very fast so that it charred but remained crunchy, a textural contrast to the sweet softness of the grilled eggplant. The light char unites the two vegetables.

The eggplants should be thin, no more than 2½ inches in diameter. If they are thicker, they will take a very long time to cook. Look for small Italian or Asian varieties. And the heat should be medium to medium-low, depending on thickness—the thicker the eggplant, the lower the heat—or they will burn before they are cooked through. The kale is kneaded slightly to tenderize it. **SERVES 4**

FOR THE EGGPLANTS

4 small, narrow eggplants, about 8 ounces each
¼ cup extra virgin olive oil, plus more for brushing
Coarse salt and freshly ground black pepper
¼ cup fresh lemon juice
1 elephant garlic clove (or 2 large regular garlic cloves), minced
1 tablespoon red wine vinegar
1 small bunch curly kale, stems and tough center ribs removed, torn into bite-sized pieces
1 bunch Tuscan (black) kale, tough stems removed

FOR THE FISH

4 small whole fish, such as branzino or snapper, about 1 pound each, cleaned
About ½ cup extra virgin olive oil
Coarse salt and freshly ground black pepper
2 small fennel bulbs, trimmed, cored, and sliced very thin on a mandoline
1 bunch scallions, trimmed and chopped

To make the eggplant, cut them lengthwise almost in half to butterfly them, keeping them attached in the middle. Open them up and lightly score the cut sides with a sharp knife.

Heat a charcoal grill or two ridged cast-iron grill pans over medium heat. Brush the grill or pans generously with olive oil. Set the opened eggplants skin side down on the grill, press them down slightly with a spatula, and let them cook slowly for 10 to 15 minutes, depending on their thickness, until they are softened and nicely charred on the bottom. Brush the cut sides generously with olive oil and season with salt and pepper. Brush the grill with more oil, turn the eggplants cut side down, and cook for another 10 to 15 minutes, until they are nicely marked and very tender. Transfer to a platter, opened skin side down.

While the eggplant is grilling, start the fish: Make diagonal slashes on both sides of each fish, about ¾ inch apart. Brush with olive oil and season with salt and pepper. Stuff the sliced fennel into the slashes on both sides of each fish. Drizzle a little more olive oil on top, making sure the fish and exposed fennel are well oiled. Set aside.

Whisk together the ¼ cup olive oil, lemon juice, garlic, red wine vinegar, and salt and pepper to taste in a small bowl. Pour half of this over the kale in a large bowl and, using your hands, toss the kale in the vinaigrette, vigorously kneading the dressing into the leaves to tenderize them. Reserve the remaining vinaigrette.

Using tongs, arrange the kale on the hot grill. When the edges are slightly browned, about 2 minutes, drizzle with more dressing and turn to the other side. When the edges are browned and crisp, pile the kale onto the opened eggplants and fold them closed, as you would a sandwich. Press down lightly to compress them, then slice on the diagonal into pieces about 2 inches wide.

Brush the grill grate or grill pans well with oil. When it is smoking hot, arrange the fish on the grate or pans and grill, without moving it, for about 7 minutes, or until the bottom of the fish is nicely marked. (You can carefully lift the tail to check.) Turn the fish over carefully with a fish turner or two wide spatulas and grill the other side for about 7 more minutes. The fish is done when the flesh is opaque throughout and releases easily from the bone.

Transfer the fish to a serving platter, drizzle with olive oil, and scatter the chopped scallions over the top. Serve immediately, with the grilled eggplant and kale sandwiches.

WHEN MY FISH STICKS

For those of you who say, "Sounds good, but when I grill a whole fish it always sticks to the grate," my answer is, mine often does too. Fish skin has an innate lust to become one with anything you grill it on. A clean, hot grill swabbed generously with oil before grilling can help, but often fish actually doesn't pull away cleanly from the grill. The fish still tastes wonderful.

When grilling fillets, make sure the grill is absolutely clean, and oil both it and the fish well to prevent sticking. When you swab the grill with oil, use tongs to hold your paper towel or cloth so you don't get burned if some of the oil drips onto the coals and they flare up. Use one or two wide sharp-edged spatulas for turning (or consider other tools that might work, like a pastry scraper or the bottom of a metal tart pan). Whether whole or in fillets, look at the fish from the side with your eyes at grill level—you will be able to see what is happening at the edges without lifting it. When it looks browned as if it wants to release, pick up the tail end or a corner to check. If it resists, check again in 30 seconds or so.

Grilled Chilean Sea Bass with Toasted Almond Salsa

A piece of well-grilled fish, cut with a fork, comes apart like the petals of a tulip, while a poorly grilled fish forever loses its subtle texture. I learned this truth many years ago from my dear friend Guzmán Artagaveytia, who was born and raised within sight of the lighthouse of José Ignacio, in Uruguay. I had recently started to cook with fires and could not imagine how the infernal heat that I cooked with would not destroy a piece of fish. Guzmán told me: You must watch over your fish as you would a newborn child while it naps.

I've made this recipe with Chilean sea bass and grouper as well as sea trout, which is also called weakfish in the North of the United States or speckled trout in the South. It is quite delicious and is not even distantly related to any trout that Izaak Walton might have gone for. It will also work with any firm-fleshed fish, such as striper, redfish, and the underrated bluefish, which is sublime when freshly caught. **SERVES 4**

About 6 tablespoons extra virgin olive oil, plus more for drizzling
1½ pounds Chilean sea bass fillet, skin on, in one piece
12 fresh sage leaves
Coarse sea salt and freshly ground black pepper
Toasted Almond Salsa (recipe follows) or Salsa Llajua (page 284)

Heat a charcoal grill or a large cast-iron grill pan over high heat. Brush the grill grate or pan generously with olive oil. Brush both sides of the fish well with olive oil. Arrange the sage leaves on the flesh side, patting them down so they adhere. Sprinkle with salt and pepper.

Invert the fish, sage side down, onto the grill, and grill, without moving it, for 7 to 10 minutes, depending on the thickness, until it is nicely marked. Brush the skin again with oil. Check to see if the fish is ready to turn by lifting up the tail end or one edge—when it is ready, it will release easily. Carefully slide a wide sharp-edged spatula between the fish and the grill (you can use a second one on the other side of the fish if necessary) and flip the fish. Cook on the other side for 5 to 7 minutes, adjusting the heat if necessary, until the skin is crisp and the fish is just cooked through. Transfer to a serving platter and drizzle with olive oil.

Serve immediately, with the salsa.

NOTE: These timings are for a 1½-pound fish fillet in one piece. If the fillet is cut into smaller pieces, these will cook in less time.

Toasted Almond Salsa
MAKES ABOUT 1½ CUPS

½ cup blanched whole almonds
½ cup finely chopped fresh flat-leaf parsley
Grated zest and juice of 1 lemon
½ cup extra virgin olive oil
Coarse salt and freshly ground black pepper
Crushed red pepper flakes (optional)

Heat the oven to 350°F. Spread the almonds out on a baking sheet and toast in the oven for about 10 minutes, stirring them once or twice and rotating the pan occasionally if they are browning unevenly. When they are fragrant and light gold in color, transfer to a plate to cool completely.

Finely chop the nuts and transfer to a medium bowl. Add the parsley, lemon zest, and juice, then gradually whisk in the olive oil. Season to taste with salt, pepper, and, if desired, crushed red pepper flakes.

Grilled Chilean Sea Bass with Toasted Almond Salsa (page 181).

Grilled Giant Flatfish Stuffed with Peppers, Onions, and Herbs

The age-old challenge when grilling fish is how to prevent it from sticking. Personally, I don't care if it sticks a little as I remove it from the grill, but I will admit it looks prettier if it doesn't. The solution when you are grilling a whole stuffed fish is to use a very large, flat grill basket; line up a pair of large baskets, side by side, or put the fish between two jerky racks. You can rig them together using wire and a pair of pliers. The juiciness of the fish and the drama of its char-grilled look is worth the trouble.

You need a fairly large fish so the peppers and onions have time to cook. Fluke, halibut, or turbot are all good candidates. The ingredients and timing below are for a 5½-pound fish, the smallest size I recommend for this method.

To serve, cover a table with several thicknesses of brown paper, lay the whole fish on it, drizzle with olive oil, and invite your guests to dig in. **SERVES 6 TO 8**

1 red onion

2 lemons

1 pound red and green frying peppers, sliced very thin

6 garlic cloves, finely chopped

1 whole flatfish (see headnote), 5½ pounds cleaned weight, at room temperature

Coarse salt and freshly ground black pepper

About 2 cups extra virgin olive oil, plus more for drizzling

2 cups dry white wine

Heat a grill over a medium fire. Thinly slice the red onion on a mandoline, then thinly slice the lemons on it. Combine the onion, lemons, peppers, and garlic in a bowl, tossing well.

Lay a length of foil on a work surface. Rinse the fish inside and out, pat it dry with paper towels, and lay it on the foil with the top (thicker) side up. Trace a line with your finger down the center of the fish to locate the backbone and then, with a sharp knife, cut down the length of the bone. Insert the knife between the flesh and the backbone, and carefully separate the flesh from the small bones to make the first of four pockets. Repeat on the other side of the backbone to make the second pocket on that side of the fish.

Salt and pepper the pockets. Distribute one-quarter of the sliced vegetables and garlic inside each pocket, along the whole length. Drizzle the vegetables with olive oil and a little of the white wine and season with salt and pepper. Pat the pockets closed and brush the skin generously with olive oil. Use the foil to carefully turn the fish over onto a board, without losing any stuffing. Then make two other pockets on this side of the fish and stuff with the remaining vegetables.

Cut 3 or more slits deep into the fins and several inches apart so you can slide lengths of butcher's twine through them. Cut the same number of lengths of twine, double the width of the fish with at least 6 inches left over. Slide a piece of twine beneath the center of the fish, bring up the ends through the slits on either side, and tie them together just tightly enough to hold the pockets closed. Coat the skin of the fish with olive oil again.

Open a very large grill basket, or two of them side by side, or lay out one of two large jerky racks (see Note) and brush well with oil. Lay the fish on top and close the grill basket(s), or cover with the second oiled rack. Secure the baskets or racks with wire or butcher's twine.

Lay the enclosed fish top side down on the grill, douse it through the rack with half the remaining white wine, and grill for about 15 minutes, or until the fish is crisp and brown on the bottom—the aroma will alert you when that side is almost done. When the thickest part of the flesh on the bottom side has just turned opaque, turn the basket(s) or racks over on the grill and douse the other side of the fish with the remaining white wine. Grill for another 15 minutes and check for doneness: The flesh should be pearly and opaque and should release easily from the bone but should still be very moist, with an internal temperature of about 140°F. Carry the enclosed fish to the paper-lined table and open the basket(s) or remove the top rack.

To serve, lift portions of fish and vegetables off the bone with a spatula onto plates. Serve with olive oil on the side for drizzling.

NOTE: A pair of Camp Chef jerky racks (see Some Important Tools, page 294) works very well for a large fish like this.

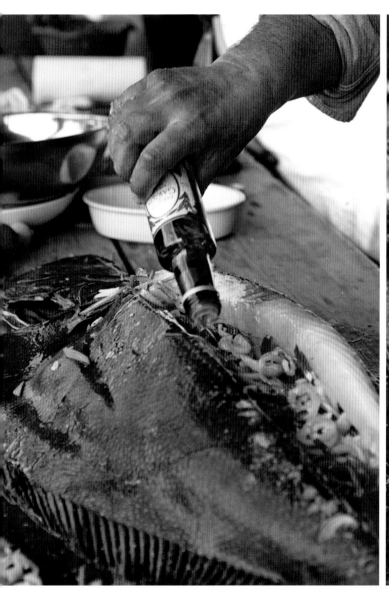

Grilled Dover Sole
with Parsleyed Boiled Potatoes

Flatfish, whether the lordly Dover sole or the more economical flounder and other family members, present a challenge to many grillers. Indoors, it's not practical to cook more than one whole Dover sole. Outdoors, on a big grill, you have room to do as many as you can fit. **SERVES 1**

About ¼ cup extra virgin olive oil

1 whole Dover sole, about 1¼ pounds, cleaned

3 fingerling or other small potatoes, boiled in their skins and kept warm

Coarse salt and freshly ground black pepper

2 tablespoons chopped fresh flat-leaf parsley

2 scallions, trimmed and chopped

Lemon wedges

Heat a charcoal grill or a large ridged grill pan big enough for the fish over medium-high heat. Brush a large plate with olive oil and keep it handy. Brush both the fish and the grill or pan generously with olive oil. When the oil starts to smoke, set the fish on the grill or pan and cook, without moving it, for about 7 minutes. Lift the tail end slightly to check it. If the fish is nicely marked and crisp on the bottom and lifts easily from the grill, it is ready to turn. If not, give it a minute or so more. Carefully slide a wide sharp-edged spatula or the bottom of a tart pan under the fish, to lift it with as little damage to the skin as possible, and, in one quick motion, flip the fish over onto the plate. Brush the grill or pan with more oil, then slide the fish back onto the grill and cook the other side for another 5 minutes or so, until the skin is crisp and the fish is cooked through.

While the fish is cooking, tear the potatoes into 2 or 3 pieces each.

Transfer the fish to a platter and surround with the torn potatoes. Season the fish and potatoes with salt and pepper, scatter the parsley and scallions over them, and drizzle with olive oil. Serve with lemon wedges.

NOTE: Do not refrigerate the potatoes. Boil them gently while the fish is cooking, or if you have to do them before going out to the grill, keep them at room temperature.

Dover Sole, by the Alexander III Bridge over the Seine.

The boatmen in Chubut, Patagonia, brought in some fish, and I cooked them on this homemade rig that one of the local fishermen made for me.

Hake Steaks a la Plancha with Fried Potatoes and Garlic

Fish steaks—we call them *postas*—are thick enough to develop a crust but still stay juicy, especially next to the bone. Here they are served with seared lemon slices with sage and crisp potatoes in garlic-flavored oil. *Merluza blanca* (hake) from the Patagonian coast is ideal for this preparation, but any firm-fleshed white fish, such as halibut, striped bass, or redfish, will be fine. SERVES 4

2 lemons

About ½ cup extra virgin olive oil

2 garlic cloves, minced

8 large fresh sage leaves, roughly torn into pieces

Fleur de sel

Freshly ground black pepper

2 Idaho (baking) potatoes, well scrubbed

4 hake steaks, about 8 ounces each and 1 inch thick, or 2 halibut steaks, about 1 pound each and 1 inch thick

Slice the lemons ⅛ inch thick on a mandoline; set aside. Combine ¼ cup of the olive oil with the minced garlic in a small bowl.

Heat a *chapa* or two large cast-iron griddles over high heat. Coat the surface generously with olive oil. Distribute the lemon slices evenly over the surface and scatter the torn sage over them. Season with fleur de sel and pepper. The lemon slices will brown up quickly, in a minute or two. Transfer them to a plate and set aside.

Meanwhile, slice the potatoes ⅛ inch thick on the mandoline; set aside.

Coat both sides of the fish with the garlic oil and set it on the hot surface. When it is golden brown and crisp on the bottom, about 4 minutes, transfer to a separate plate. (The second side will be cooked after the potatoes go on.)

The *chapa* will now be nicely seasoned with garlic, lemon, and oil. Wipe away any small bits that look as if they will burn. Add about a tablespoon more oil, and when it shimmers, add the potatoes in a single layer (cook them in batches if necessary and keep them warm in a low oven), adding more oil as needed. When they are crisp and golden brown on one side, turn them, making room for the fish, and place the hake cooked side up next to them. Cook for another 2 or 3 minutes, until the fish has just turned opaque but is still very moist and the potatoes are tender. Transfer the steaks to a platter as they are done, arranging them in the center. Arrange the lemon slices on top and the potatoes around them. Serve immediately.

Slashed-and-Stuffed Black Sea Bass with Potatoes, Leeks, and Mushrooms

I often cook with this slash-and-stuff method when I catch wild brook trout on The Island. When I came across some lovely large branzino in Paris, I gave them the same treatment on my traveling grill. The slashes holding the sliced red onions and lemon become islands of complementary flavor in the midst of the mild flesh of the fish.

I made this recipe last year in the tiny place de Furstenberg in Saint-Germain-des-Prés. When I first worked in Paris, I used to spend whole afternoons there in the Musée Delacroix, in the former home of the great Romantic artist. I would have loved to have served this to him. Maybe he would have left a little sketch of it on a napkin. **SERVES 4**

1 whole black sea bass, about 4 pounds, cleaned
About ¼ cup extra virgin olive oil, plus more
    for drizzling
2 lemons
1 red onion
Sea salt and freshly ground black pepper
3 or 4 large sprigs of flat-leaf parsley, torn
1 cup mixed pitted green and black olives,
    roughly chopped

Heat a charcoal grill over medium heat. Using a sharp knife, make 4 or 5 diagonal slashes on each side of the sea bass. Brush generously all over with the olive oil.

Slice the lemons very thin on a mandoline, and do the same with the onion. Stuff the lemon, onion slices, and parsley into the slashes in the fish. Season with salt and pepper.

Grill the fish slowly on the first side, without moving it, for about 25 minutes, until it is nicely browned and crisp on the bottom and the tail lifts easily, without sticking. Carefully slide two spatulas underneath it and flip it to cook the other side, about 15 minutes more. When the flesh has turned opaque at the thickest part of the bone, it is done. Transfer to a platter, scatter the olives over it, and drizzle with olive oil. Serve immediately, with the potatoes, leek, and mushrooms.

Potatoes, Leek, and Mushrooms

6 small potatoes
4 tablespoons unsalted butter
2 tablespoons extra virgin olive oil
1 leek, white part only, thinly sliced
1 very large shallot, minced
12 ounces cèpes (porcini) or other mushrooms,
    cleaned, trimmed, and sliced about ⅓ inch thick
1 teaspoon minced fresh thyme
1 bay leaf
salt and freshly ground pepper
¼ cup fresh flat-leaf parsley leaves, roughly
    chopped

Cover the potatoes with cold water in a saucepan and bring to a low boil. Cook gently for about 5 minutes, until half cooked, and drain. Peel the potatoes, slice about ¼ thick, and pat dry.

Melt half the butter with the olive oil in a large skillet over medium-low heat. Add the leek and shallot and sauté until translucent, about 6 minutes. Add the potatoes, mushrooms, thyme, and bay leaf and cook for about 30 minutes, stirring occasionally with a wooden spoon to redistribute the vegetables and make sure they are not sticking. Add the remaining butter as it is absorbed.

When the mushrooms and potatoes are tender and slightly browned, season to taste with salt and pepper, stir in the parsley, and serve.

NOTE: It is not practical to grill fish of this size indoors.

Slashed and stuffed *loup de mer*, also known as branzino. In America, it's hard to find large branzino, and it's usually farmed. If you prefer wild fish, as I do, sea bass is the way to go. (See recipe on page 193.)

Prawns, Sardines, and Anchovies a la Plancha with Zucchini, Swiss Chard, and Minted Yogurt

This is a spectacular dish and as flavorful as anything you can make. I often encourage people to eat more little fish, like sardines and anchovies. We must stop eating only fish at the top of the food chain, or soon they will all be gone. And the little ones are so delicious. They are strong flavored, so here I balance them with a creamy, minty yogurt sauce and a side dish of chard and zucchini.

Use head-on prawns or shrimp if you can find them—they are more flavorful. The trick here is the placement of the shrimp, sardines, and anchovies on the *chapa* so they will all be ready at the same time. The anchovies are tiny, so they are arranged around the outside, which is cooler. Since seafood cooks very quickly, have the mint sauce chilled and the vegetables ready before you start grilling.

SERVES 4

FOR THE SEAFOOD
12 prawns or jumbo shrimp
Extra virgin olive oil for brushing
Coarse salt and freshly ground black pepper
4 fresh sardines, about 8 ounces, cleaned
12 fresh anchovies, about 8 ounces, cleaned

FOR THE MINT YOGURT SAUCE
1 cup fresh mint leaves, finely chopped
1 cup Greek yogurt

FOR THE ZUCCHINI AND CHARD
2 small zucchini, trimmed
3 tablespoons extra virgin olive oil
8 garlic cloves, thinly sliced
1 large shallot, thinly sliced
2 ounces pancetta, chopped
12 large Swiss chard leaves, stems and tough
  center stalks removed and leaves sliced
  crosswise into thin strips

To clean the prawns or shrimps, using kitchen shears, make a shallow cut into the back of each shell where it meets the head to locate the black digestive tract. Then cut down the length of the shell and pull out the strip with your finger or the tip of a knife, leaving the shell attached. Rinse under cold water and pat thoroughly dry.

To make the sauce, stir the chopped mint into the yogurt in a small bowl, mixing well to combine. Cover with plastic wrap and refrigerate until ready to serve.

To prepare the zucchini and chard, using a mandoline, slice the zucchini lengthwise into thin ribbons, laying them out on paper towels to keep them separated; pat them dry before cooking.

Heat a *chapa* or a large cast-iron griddle over medium heat. Add a tablespoon of olive oil and sauté the garlic and shallot, stirring occasionally, until lightly browned. Transfer to a large bowl and set aside. Wipe off the hot surface with a paper towel to remove any remaining bits of garlic or shallot. Add the pancetta, with another tablespoon of oil, and sauté for 2 minutes to start rendering the fat. Carefully stir in the zucchini ribbons and cook for several minutes, stirring occasionally, until the pancetta is crisp and the zucchini is lightly browned. Transfer to the bowl with the garlic and shallot and stir gently.

Add the remaining tablespoon of oil to the hot surface and sauté the chard for a minute or two, until it softens. Add the zucchini mixture and stir gently to combine with the chard, then return to the bowl until ready to serve.

Surf and Swine

Heat the clean *chapa* or two large cast-iron griddles over high heat for at least 5 minutes. Open out the prawns, shell side down, flattening them with a spatula to keep them open. Brush them on both sides with olive oil and season with salt and pepper. Pat the sardines and anchovies dry and brush them with olive oil.

Brush the *chapa* generously with olive oil. When the oil shimmers, set the prawns shell side down about an inch apart on the *chapa* or on one griddle; if your griddle is small, do this in batches. Cook for about 4 minutes, or until the shells are a golden pink and crisp and the flesh is almost opaque. Using tongs, turn the prawns and quickly gild the other side to finish cooking. Transfer to a serving platter.

Meanwhile, arrange the sardines, also about an inch apart, elsewhere on the *chapa* or on the second griddle. Cook for 2½ minutes, or until they are crisp and browned on the bottom. Turn and cook for about 2 minutes on the other side, adding more oil if necessary, until the flesh is opaque and will separate easily from the bone. As soon as you turn the sardines, arrange the anchovies around the edges of the *chapa* or the griddle. The anchovies will cook in about 1 minute per side. As the fish is done, arrange on the serving platter with the shrimp. Meanwhile, reheat the zucchini and chard in a small skillet.

Heap the zucchini and chard on the platter and serve immediately, with the mint yogurt sauce.

I have always been struck by the affinity between seafood and ham, bacon, or sausage. One day, in the shadow of the old abandoned Lighthouse of the Lions just off the coast of Chubut, Jorge Kriege brought us some gorgeous *escrofalo,* a pumpkin-seed-shaped fish. I slashed them, stuffed some prosciutto into the incisions, and threw them on an oiled *chapa*. Topped with olives and capers, the result was piquant, salty, smoky, and, of course, fishy. Any fish this size will work. **SERVES 4**

1 whole sea bass, about 1¾ pounds, cleaned
4 thin slices prosciutto, torn in half
6 tablespoons extra virgin olive oil
⅓ cup mild black olives, pitted
1 tablespoon capers, rinsed
Lemon wedges

Hold the fish dorsal side up (as though it were swimming) on a work surface and, using a sharp serrated knife, make 3 or 4 cuts about 1½ inches deep and 1 inch apart straight across the back of the fish. Fold the prosciutto loosely in half and insert as much as you can of it into the cuts, letting the excess drape attractively. Brush the fish all over with 1½ tablespoons of the olive oil.

Pat the olives and capers dry. Chop coarsely. Combine in a small bowl and set aside.

Heat a *chapa* or a large cast-iron griddle over medium heat. Brush with a spoon of oil. When the oil shimmers, add the fish and cook for about 8 minutes, without moving it, until the skin and prosciutto on the first side are crisp. Using a sharp-edged wide spatula, turn the fish over, spooning a little more olive oil under it, and cook on the other side until the flesh turns opaque throughout, about 7 more minutes. Transfer to a serving platter.

Drizzle the fish with the remaining olive oil, scatter the olives and capers over it, and serve immediately, with lemon wedges.

PICTURED ON PAGE 198

Chupin de Pescado

A *chupin* is a fish stew, traditionally made by the Indians in the north of Argentina. I am indebted to them for the cooking lessons given me over many campfires in the wilds of their homeland. The name *chupin* comes from the Spanish *chupar,* a word one uses when something is so delicious that you say, *"Hasta que chupar los dedos,"* which means "finger-licking good." I love a cod chupin, but hake, grouper, or any similar firm-fleshed white fish works well. **SERVES 6**

½ **cup extra virgin olive oil, plus more for drizzling**

2 **onions, finely chopped**

8 **garlic cloves, finely chopped**

1 **large fennel bulb, trimmed, cored, and diced**

1 **tablespoon pimentón dulce (sweet Spanish paprika)**

1 **large red chile pepper, cut lengthwise in half and seeds removed**

1 **cup dry white wine**

2 **bay leaves**

1 **tablespoon chopped fresh oregano**

6 **cups Rich Vegetable Stock (page 288)**

2 **red or Yukon Gold potatoes, peeled and cut into ½-inch pieces**

Coarse salt and freshly ground black pepper

8 **ounces green beans, topped and tailed**

2¼ **pounds thick cod or other firm white fish steaks**

3 **large ripe tomatoes, chopped (or 2 cups chopped canned plum tomatoes)**

¼ **cup fresh lemon juice**

1 **teaspoon crushed red pepper flakes, plus more for serving**

1 **small bunch Swiss chard, stems removed and leaves cut crosswise into thin strips**

Heat ¼ cup of the olive oil in a large Dutch oven over medium-low heat. Add the chopped onion, garlic, fennel, and pimentón and sauté until the vegetables are softened and starting to turn golden. Add the chile pepper and white wine, raise the heat to medium-high, and boil until the wine reduces by half. Add the bay leaves and oregano, pour in the vegetable stock, and return to a boil. Reduce the heat to low, add the potatoes, and cook for about 5 minutes, or until the potatoes are half cooked. Season with salt and pepper.

Meanwhile, cut the green beans into bite-size pieces and blanch them in a saucepan of boiling salted water for about a minute, until they are bright green but still crisp. Drain in a sieve and run under cold water to stop the cooking. Set aside.

Add the fish and chopped tomatoes to the pot and simmer gently until the fish flakes easily from the bone, about 5 minutes or so. Remove from the heat and let cool slightly.

Use a slotted spoon to transfer the fish to a bowl, then remove the bones and skin. Return the fish to the soup and stir in the remaining ¼ cup olive oil and the lemon juice. Season carefully with salt, pepper, and the red pepper flakes.

To serve, return the soup to a boil, add the green beans and chard, and cook for a minute or two, until the chard is just tender. Ladle into soup bowls and serve with olive oil and red pepper flakes on the side.

PRECEDING: Surf and Swine (page 197) with Eggplant a la Plancha with Cherry Tomatoes and Anchovies (page 213).

Mussels Steamed in Red Wine–Butter Sauce with Shallots and Parsley

Cooking mussels in white wine is a delicious tradition, but you don't always have to baby your mussels with white wine. They have a deep briny flavor and the fortitude to stand up to red wine too. In addition to the traditional garlic, I use shallots, sautéed and cooked in a golden roux. The result is a rich, velvety sauce. To mop it up, instead of a baguette, try some dark bread, which will add to the powerful flavor of the wine sauce. **SERVES 4**

8 tablespoons (1 stick) unsalted butter
⅔ cup minced shallots
4 garlic cloves, minced
2 tablespoons all-purpose flour
2 cups light red wine
4 fresh thyme sprigs
Coarse salt and freshly ground black pepper
4 pounds mussels, scrubbed if necessary, any
    cracked or open ones discarded
1 cup finely chopped fresh flat-leaf parsley
Crusty bread

Melt the butter in a large Dutch oven over low heat. Add the shallots and sauté gently for 2 or 3 minutes, until they soften. Add the garlic and sauté for 1 minute. Stir in the flour to form a roux and cook, stirring, for about 5 minutes, until it turns a light blond color.

Gradually stir in the red wine, using a wooden spoon. Add the thyme, raise the heat to medium, and bring to a gentle boil, stirring. Continue cooking for about 5 minutes, stirring occasionally, until the alcohol cooks off and the mixture thickens enough to lightly coat the spoon. Season to taste with salt and pepper.

Add the mussels and half the parsley, stir, cover, and cook for 2 to 3 minutes, depending on the size of the mussels. Remove the lid and transfer any mussels that have opened wide to a large bowl. Give the rest of the mussels a stir to redistribute them, replace the lid, and cook for several minutes longer, shaking the pot from time to time to move the mussels around, and checking every minute or so to remove them as they are done. Discard any that refuse to open.

Off the heat, return the cooked mussels, in their shells, to the sauce and stir to coat. Stir in the remaining parsley and ladle into soup bowls, with plenty of sauce. Serve with slices of crusty bread.

Octopus in an Iron Box with Chard, Green Beans, Tomatoes, and Eggs

I often prepare this recipe in cast-iron boxes of the type that I first saw in Brazil. They make for a terrific presentation, but a big cast-iron skillet, griddle, or brazier will do just as well. You want an octopus of about two pounds, which has tentacles large enough to give you a crunchy outside and tender flesh inside. Too big, and they are invariably tough, while the small ones are all crunch and no chew. **SERVES 4**

Coarse sea salt
1 octopus, about 2 pounds
2 onions, cut in half
2 carrots
12 black peppercorns
About 1 cup extra virgin olive oil
2 heads garlic, cut horizontally in half
1 bunch Swiss chard, stems removed
12 ounces green beans, topped and tailed
24 cherry tomatoes
12 small potatoes, boiled in their skins
4 large eggs
Freshly ground black pepper
Salsa Provenzal (page 288)

Pour water into a stockpot until it is a little more than half full and salt the water. Bring it to a boil and, holding the octopus by the head, plunge it into the water for about 10 seconds, then pull it out. Bring the water back to a boil and repeat twice more.

Add the onions, carrots, and peppercorns to the water and reduce the heat to a low simmer. Return the octopus to the pot and simmer for 30 minutes, then turn the heat off and let stand for 30 minutes, then bring back to a simmer and repeat the process. It should be done once for each pound of octopus. Let cool in the liquid.

Separate the head of the octopus from the tentacles and discard. If not cooking immediately, wrap the tentacles in plastic wrap and refrigerate. Bring to room temperature before charring.

Heat four individual iron boxes or as many cast-iron skillets or griddles as you have over medium-high heat. Brush the surfaces with oil, and when it shimmers, add the halved garlic heads, cut side down. Let them brown and soften for several minutes, then rub them over the hot surfaces to flavor them and move them to the side. Add the octopus tentacles to one box. When they are crisp and slightly charred on one side, after about 2 minutes, drizzle them with oil and turn them. Meanwhile, quickly cook the chard, green beans, tomatoes, and potatoes in the same way, keeping the items separate and drizzling them with olive oil to keep them moist.

Clear a space in each box or pan, add a little more oil, and fry the eggs.

Divide the vegetables, octopus, and eggs among four boxes or individual dinner plates and serve immediately, with the salsa.

Split Lobster a la Parrilla with Scallops

Many people cook lobster on a grill by splitting it and placing it meat side down: This method is guaranteed to dry out and toughen the meat. I place the lobster shell side down on the *parrilla* so that it poaches quickly in its own juices, basted with butter and tarragon. As for the scallops, they are more delicate and require less cooking, so they are sautéed briefly in butter at the end. By all means, use scallops with roe if you can get them. The roe is much loved in France, but I rarely see it elsewhere. Its combination of creaminess and tang is intense but very pleasing. **SERVES 2**

1 live lobster, about 1½ pounds
8 tablespoons (1 stick) unsalted butter, at room
    temperature
¼ cup finely chopped fresh tarragon
8 ounces scallops, preferably with roe attached
Fleur de sel
Lemon wedges

Heat a charcoal grill over medium-high heat.

Set the lobster belly side down on a cutting board and hold it down firmly by the tail with a kitchen towel. Plunge a sharp chef's knife into the base of the head just above the point where it meets the back, to kill the lobster instantly, then pull the knife toward you and continue cutting to split the head in half. Turn the lobster around and cut down the length of the tail to split it in two. Remove the sand sac from the head and the gray intestinal vein from the tail and discard. Set the lobster aside.

Melt half the butter in a small saucepan, add the tarragon, and stir to combine. Keep warm on the grill.

When the coals are ready, place the lobster halves shell side down on the grill and baste the meat with the tarragon butter. Grill, basting occasionally, until the shells turn bright red and the flesh is opaque throughout, 10 to 12 minutes. Transfer to a large platter.

Meanwhile, set a *chapa* or a cast-iron griddle on the grill next to the lobster and melt 2 tablespoons of the remaining butter in it. Pat the scallops dry with paper towels, and when the butter foams, arrange the scallops on the griddle in a single layer. Cook them, without moving them, for about 2 minutes, until they brown lightly on one side. Turn them carefully, add the rest of the butter, and cook for another minute or so, depending on the size of the scallops. They should be just opaque throughout, with the roe, if you have it, still creamy. Sprinkle with fleur de sel and transfer to the platter with the lobster.

Serve immediately, with lemon wedges and fleur de sel.

Two large lobsters in the kitchen of the Uxua Casa Hotel in Trancoso.

VEGETABLES AND BEANS

Braised Carrots

Carrots are universal: they go with anything. This is the most uncomplicated of braises, with a spectrum of beautiful flavor notes. The carrots accept them, and elevate them, but still retain their essential flavor. **SERVES 4 TO 6**

2 pounds young carrots, trimmed, leaving a bit of green, and peeled
3 cups Rich Vegetable Stock (page 288)
1 cup dry white wine
2 garlic cloves, smashed and peeled
4 large bushy fresh thyme sprigs
1 bay leaf
6 black peppercorns
Coarse salt
Freshly ground black pepper
Extra virgin olive oil for drizzling

Heat an *horno* or the oven to 375°F.

   If some carrots are much thicker than others, halve them lengthwise so they will all cook evenly. Lay them in a single layer in a small roasting pan. Add the stock, wine, garlic, thyme, bay leaf, and peppercorns and sprinkle lightly with salt. Cover tightly with foil and bake for 30 to 40 minutes, or until the carrots are very tender. Transfer the carrots to a wide serving dish and keep warm.

   With the back of a fork, crush the garlic cloves and thyme into the cooking liquid. Set the roasting pan over medium heat for a minute or two, stirring, to concentrate the flavor; adjust the seasoning with salt and pepper. Strain.

   Spoon the liquid over the carrots, drizzle lightly with olive oil, and serve.

Baby Turnips a la Plancha with Sun-Dried Tomatoes

Everyone loves babies. Baby turnips are no exception for me. They always have beautifully tender leaves too. When you split them lengthwise and grill them slowly on a *chapa,* they caramelize nicely. For decades I've gotten my vegetables from the incomparable Sergio Chaben, who sells them from his truck in Buenos Aires. After twenty years, he still can be trusted to find something special. I like his truck because it is old and beat-up but obviously well loved. It is so ancient and timeworn that it is the color of no color, and I have absolutely no idea what kind of truck it is. **SERVES 4**

1 pound baby turnips, with leaves attached, or small Japanese turnips
1 red onion
1 tablespoon extra virgin olive oil
8 slices Sun-Dried Tomatoes (page 285)

Slice the turnips in half from root to stem, or quarter them if larger. Thinly slice the red onion on a mandoline.

   Heat a *chapa* or a large cast-iron griddle over low heat. Brush with the oil. Arrange the turnips on the hot surface, cut side down. Scatter the sliced onion over them and top with the sun-dried tomatoes. Cook for about 8 minutes, until the turnips are browned on the bottom and tender, turning any quartered ones to brown both cut sides. Toss and serve.

ALSO PICTURED ON PAGES 210–211

Eggplant a la Plancha
with Cherry Tomatoes and Anchovies

There are few things I like less than undercooked eggplants: they are tough and bitter, and I think undercooking is the reason many people despair of making them on the grill. But when cooked properly, they are soft, creamy, and delicious. I start with small to medium eggplants, which are more tender to begin with, and then slice them fairly thin, so they will cook all the way through on the *chapa* relatively quickly while developing a pleasing char.

Eggplants, as Italians discovered centuries ago, play very nicely with tomatoes—which scientists tell us are their biological cousins. You may think this recipe calls for too many anchovies. Trust me, they are brilliant with the eggplant. **SERVES 4**

About ½ cup extra virgin olive oil

1 large garlic clove, minced

2 medium eggplants, about 10 ounces each

Coarse salt and freshly ground black pepper

8 ounces cherry tomatoes, cut in half

6 ounces anchovies packed in olive oil, drained

Place ¼ cup of the olive oil in a small bowl and stir in the minced garlic.

Cut off the stem end of the eggplants and slice them lengthwise about ⅓ inch thick. Brush the tops of the slices with some of the garlic oil and season very lightly with salt and pepper.

Heat a *chapa* or a cast-iron griddle over medium-high heat until a drop of water hisses on the surface. Brush generously with some of the remaining plain olive oil, and when it shimmers, add the eggplant slices, oiled side down. Cook, without moving them, for about 7 minutes, or until nicely browned on the bottom. Brush generously with the garlic oil, season with salt and a few grinds of pepper, and turn, adding more olive oil to the *chapa* if necessary. Cook on the other side for about 6 minutes, or until the eggplant is crisp, browned, and very tender when pierced with a fork. Transfer to a wide serving platter. You may cook the eggplant in batches.

Meanwhile, brush another part of the *chapa* or another hot griddle generously with olive oil. When it shimmers, add the tomatoes, cut side down, about 1 inch apart. Cook the tomatoes, without disturbing them, for about 3 minutes, or until they are nicely charred on the bottom. Transfer to the serving platter, arranging them over the eggplant.

Roughly chop the anchovies and scatter over the eggplant and tomatoes. Drizzle with more olive oil, season to taste with pepper, and serve hot or at room temperature.

ALSO PICTURED ON PAGE 198

Eggplants Stuffed with Tomatoes and Cuartirolo Cheese

You want fresh, firm, sweet eggplants with as few seeds as possible for this recipe. Huge eggplants won't do. If the eggplants you get do have a significant proportion of seeds, salt them and allow to drain for 20 minutes, as described below, to draw out any bitter juices and improve the texture. In Argentina, cuartirolo, originally an Italian cheese, is my preference for this dish, but somehow the Italians who immigrated to North America (usually from the same areas as the Italo-Argentine community) forgot to pack any cuartirolo. Fresh mozzarella will do just fine. You can double this recipe for a main course.

SERVES 4

**2 firm medium eggplants,
    about 8 ounces each**
2 bay leaves
One 10-ounce loaf country bread, day-old
½ cup extra virgin olive oil
Coarse salt and freshly ground black pepper
2 garlic cloves, finely chopped
**6 large ripe plum tomatoes, cored and roughly
    chopped**
**10 ounces cuartirolo cheese (or substitute fresh
    mozzarella), cut into ½-inch-thick slices**

Heat an *horno* or the oven to 375°F.

Cut the eggplants lengthwise in half. With a sharp knife, trace a margin about ½ inch wide around the perimeter of each half. Using a sharp spoon, scoop out the center of each eggplant half. Roughly chop the pulp, keeping it fairly chunky. If there are a significant amount of seeds, salt both the shells and the pulp and drain in a colander for 20 minutes, then rinse off the salt and bitter juices and pat the pulp very dry with paper towels.

Pour an inch or so of water into a large skillet and add the bay leaves. Bring to a boil, add the eggplant shells, cut side down, cover, and cook over medium heat for about 8 minutes, or until tender enough to pierce with a sharp knife. Drain, pat dry with paper towels, and transfer to an oiled shallow baking dish that will hold them in one layer. Set aside.

Cut the crusts from the bread and tear the bread roughly into small pieces, about ⅓ inch across. Toss with 3 tablespoons of the olive oil in a bowl and season with salt and pepper. Set a cast-iron skillet over medium heat and, working in batches, toast the bread crumbs for about 2 minutes, until golden and crunchy, turning them as necessary and transferring to a bowl as they are done.

Wipe out the skillet, set it over medium heat, and add 2 tablespoons more oil, the garlic, and the chopped eggplant. Sauté, stirring, for about 5 minutes, until the eggplant is golden and softened. Stir in the chopped tomatoes and cook for about 5 minutes, stirring occasionally, until the tomatoes have released their juice and broken down into a thick, chunky sauce. Remove from the heat.

Fill the eggplant halves with the eggplant-tomato mixture. Divide the cheese into 4 portions and nestle into the eggplant filling. Cover with the toasted bread crumbs and drizzle with the remaining 3 tablespoons olive oil.

Bake for about 20 minutes, until the cheese is completely melted and the bread crumbs are crunchy. Serve hot.

Braised Beans
with Red Wine and Tomato

I devoted myself to beans when I opened a restaurant in the Brazilian beach town of Trancoso, where they are a fundamental part of the local diet. Instead of the traditional ham or bacon, I fortify these beans with a rich brown pork stock and plenty of red wine. Brazilians like to overcook their beans, until at least half of them have fallen apart. So the answer to the question "How long do I cook the beans?" is, "Way long."

You can use any type of dried beans, such as borlotti (cranberry), cannellini, or small limas. Or experiment with some of the many intriguing heirloom beans available in specialty stores or online, such as Tongues of Fire, a type of borlotti that originated in Tierra del Fuego. The cooking time will depend on the freshness of the batch, and sometimes it's fun to mix different types. They cook into an appealing blend, some broken, some not, in a rich elixir that we also drink as a broth. Once braised, they will keep in the fridge for several days and get even better as the flavors deepen. **SERVES 12**

1½ pounds dried beans, soaked in water overnight and drained
¼ cup extra virgin olive oil
1½ cups chopped onions
1 cup chopped celery
8 garlic cloves, chopped
4 fresh rosemary sprigs
8 fresh thyme sprigs
3 bay leaves
Two 28-ounce cans San Marzano tomatoes, roughly chopped, with their juice
4 cups Rich Brown Pork Stock (page 289), or as needed
2 cups medium-bodied red wine, such as Uruguayan Tannat
Coarse salt and freshly ground black pepper

Put the beans in a large pot, cover with water, and bring to a boil.

Meanwhile, in a large skillet, heat the olive oil over medium heat and sauté the onions and celery for about 5 minutes, until softened and translucent. Add the garlic and cook for a minute or two more. Remove from the heat.

Tie the rosemary, thyme, and bay leaves together with a piece of kitchen string.

When the beans have started to boil, skim off any foam that has risen to the top, then stir in the sautéed onion, celery, and garlic, the tomatoes, with their juice, the stock, red wine, and herbs. The beans should be covered by at least 2 inches of liquid; add more stock or hot water if needed. Bring to a boil over medium heat, skimming off any foam that rises to the surface. Once foam ceases to appear, reduce the heat to a gentle simmer and let the beans bubble slowly for anywhere from 45 minutes to 2 hours, depending on the type and freshness of the beans, until they are tender and somewhat broken. Stir the pot occasionally to make sure the beans are not drying out or sticking to the bottom, and add more stock or water if necessary.

When the beans are done, season with salt and pepper and serve.

Braised Black Beans

Whenever I cook beans outdoors, I am comforted by the sound of them bubbling in a clay pot set over the campfire. Beans are hearty and restorative, and much appreciated on a windswept day out of doors. Grilled fish, cold beer, and a plate of these beans made a complete meal one day on Bahía Bustamante, where we camped in sight of a pride of sea lions on the shore. In the distance, the first right whales of the season finished their migration of thousands of miles to their summer playground in Patagonia. A magical scene. **SERVES 4**

2 tablespoons extra virgin olive oil
1 medium onion, finely chopped
3 garlic cloves, finely chopped
5 ounces mildly smoky, slab bacon,
    roughly chopped
12 ounces dried black beans, soaked in water
    overnight and drained
1 medium carrot, quartered
2 bay leaves
6 cups Rich Vegetable Stock (page 288)
Coarse salt and freshly ground black pepper

Heat the olive oil in a large pot over medium heat. Add the onion and garlic and sauté for about 3 minutes, until they soften. Add the bacon and sauté, stirring occasionally, until it is nicely browned.

Add the beans, carrot, bay leaves, and vegetable stock, raise the heat, and bring to a boil, skimming off any foam that rises to the top. Lower the heat, partially cover the pot, and simmer for 45 minutes to 2 hours, depending on the freshness of the beans, adding more stock or hot water as needed, until the beans are tender and just beginning to break apart. The cooking liquid should be reduced and slightly thickened.

Season carefully with salt and pepper and serve hot.

Crusty Rice

Think of this as a "painless paella." By that I mean it gives you that wonderful crispy crust that is known as *soccarat* but doesn't involve having to cook lots of seafood, chicken, sausage, and the other ingredients of a classic paella, just top-quality Calasparra rice flavored with butter instead of olive oil and redolent of wine and rosemary. Trust your nose to tell you when the crust is toasted—don't allow it to overbrown or burn. **SERVES 6**

8 tablespoons (1 stick) salted butter

1 onion, finely chopped

6 garlic cloves, finely chopped

2 cups Bomba or other Calasparra rice

3½ cups Rich Vegetable Stock (page 288), or as needed

1 cup dry white wine

4 large fresh rosemary branches

Coarse salt and freshly ground black pepper

Melt the butter in a 15-inch paella pan or a wide skillet over medium-low heat. Add the onion and sauté for about 5 minutes, until softened and translucent. Add the garlic and sauté for a minute more. Sprinkle the rice evenly over the bottom of the pan and sauté for 5 minutes, turning to coat the grains.

Meanwhile, pour the stock and white wine into a saucepan and bring just to a boil. Cover and reduce to a gentle simmer.

Carefully ladle the hot liquid over the rice, arrange the rosemary branches on top, and adjust the heat so that the liquid bubbles gently. Cook for 10 to 15 minutes—do not stir the rice again, but gently shake the pan occasionally to distribute the liquid, and rotate the pan on the burner so the rice cooks evenly. When the rice has absorbed most of the liquid, taste for seasoning and adjust with salt and pepper. Turn down the heat and gently simmer for about 10 minutes more, until all the liquid is absorbed and the rice tastes almost but not quite done; add a little more hot stock or water if necessary. The grains should be separate and each grain should still have a "bite" to it.

Dunk a clean kitchen towel in hot water, wring it out, and drape it over the rice, gathering the ends of the towel up into the pan. Remove from the heat and let the rice steam for about 10 minutes.

To form the *soccarat,* return the pan to medium heat, raise the heat slightly, and cook for several minutes. Pay close attention to the aroma of the toasted rice, so as not to overbrown it. When you lift a bit of rice from the bottom, it should have a golden brown crust. Remove from the heat and serve immediately.

Creamy Polenta
with Fresh Favas and Peas

The spring season on a plate! I am a lifelong polenta lover. In 1983, I was asked to give a cooking class in Buenos Aires. We sold 150 tickets, but no one knew what I was going to teach. We handed out the recipes, which included polenta, as people filed in. And, lo and behold, they all left! Polenta was considered—by snobs and fools—a dish only for poor Italians. It is my belief that food doesn't have a class system. There is no such thing as "poor" food—the thing to avoid is poorly made food. Always bear in mind that even after you remove polenta from the heat, it will continue to absorb liquid, so if you want it to stay creamy longer, it should be very moist when you take it from the stove. It's best served immediately, piping hot. **SERVES 6**

5 to 6 cups Rich Vegetable Stock (page 288)
½ cup extra virgin olive oil
9 ounces (about 1½ cups) medium polenta
1½ cups freshly grated Parmesan, plus 2 ounces,
    shaved thin on a mandoline
1 shallot, minced
1 cup shelled, blanched, and peeled young fava
    beans
1 cup shelled baby peas
½ cup fresh mint leaves, chopped
Sea salt and freshly ground black pepper

Combine 5 cups of the vegetable stock and 2 tablespoons of the olive oil in a large saucepan and bring to a boil. Gradually stir in the polenta and continue stirring as it thickens, breaking up any lumps. Lower the heat to a simmer and cook, stirring every few minutes and adding up to 1 cup more stock as needed, until the polenta is thick and creamy but still quite moist, 15 to 20 minutes. Beat in ¼ cup more olive oil and the grated Parmesan.

Meanwhile, heat the remaining 2 tablespoons olive oil in a large skillet over medium heat. Add the shallot and sauté for several minutes, or until softened. Add the favas, peas, and mint and stir to combine. When the peas and favas are tender, just a few minutes, remove them from the heat.

When the polenta is done, briefly reheat the peas and favas and stir half into the polenta. Season carefully with salt and pepper and spoon into a warmed wide serving bowl or earthenware dish. Make a well in the center and pour the remaining peas and favas into the well and over the top. Scatter the shaved Parmesan over all and serve immediately.

Red Cabbage and Carrot Slaw

Inspired by the use of soy sauce and Napa cabbage in Asian recipes, I thought soy would work well in this brilliantly colored slaw. The lemon juice keeps the color and flavor bright. Don't grate the cabbage too fine—you want it to crunch in your mouth. Serve with Red-Wine-Braised Spareribs (page 133) for a winter meal. **SERVES 8**

FOR THE VINAIGRETTE
1 tablespoon red wine vinegar
1 tablespoon soy sauce
1 tablespoon fresh lemon juice
¼ cup olive oil
Coarse salt and freshly ground black pepper

1 pound carrots, peeled
1 pound red cabbage, cut into large wedges and cored

Whisk together the vinegar, soy sauce, and lemon juice in a small bowl. Whisking constantly, drizzle in the olive oil in a slow, steady stream. Season to taste with salt and pepper.

Grate the carrots and then the cabbage on the coarse side of an old-fashioned box grater into a bowl. Add the vinaigrette and toss well to combine. Check the seasoning and serve.

Coal-Roasted Zucchini and Swiss Chard

People are often afraid to put food directly on the coals. Never fear! Coals are actually super-clean, and the taste you pick up is beautiful. This technique works best when you have a bed of mature coals, nice and red. Before starting to cook the chard, throw one leaf on the coals so you can see how it responds to the fire before you commit. It is important that the zucchini cook all the way through. You want char on the outside and soft and creamy flesh within. Use long tongs and a grill glove. **SERVES 4**

3 young slender zucchini, trimmed
6 tablespoons extra virgin olive oil, plus more for drizzling
3 tablespoons red wine vinegar
2 teaspoons fresh thyme leaves
3 garlic cloves, thinly sliced
12 to 16 large Swiss chard leaves
Fleur de sel
Freshly ground black pepper

Prepare a bed of mature coals.

Set the zucchini directly on the coals and cook for several minutes, until charred on the bottom. Using tongs, turn to cook on another side, then continue to turn and cook on all sides until you can pierce through them with a grilling fork. Transfer to a serving platter. Cover loosely to keep warm.

Meanwhile, whisk the olive oil and vinegar in a bowl. Add the thyme and sliced garlic, then dress the leaves, as you would a salad. Pick up 3 or 4 chard leaves by the stems and set them on the coals for a minute or two, until they are half charred and half green. Cut off and discard the stems and place the chard on the platter with the zucchini. Repeat with the remaining chard in batches, arranging the leaves on the platter.

To serve, thickly slice the zucchini on the diagonal. Season the vegetables to taste with fleur de sel, pepper, and the remaining garlic-thyme vinaigrette. Serve with additional olive oil on the side for drizzling.

PICTURED ON PAGE 225

Coal-Roasted Zucchini and Swiss Chard (page 223).

Gratin of Potatoes with Emmental Wrapped in Bayonne Ham

This classic combination of favorite French ingredients is prepared in the most Argentine of cooking vessels, the *olla de barro,* a clay pot. These are made in the far north of Argentina. The trick is to make sure they are made for this purpose; not all clay pots are. Heat them very slowly and gradually, so as not to shock them or they will crack. A cast-iron pot will work if you don't have an earthenware vessel.

In France, I set up my traveling grill outside the Palais Royal in Paris and, using a clay pot, prepared my gratin with ham and truffles. You don't have to use truffles, but once a year, why not splurge on a truly sensual delicacy? As we say, *"A gozar la vida,"* which I loosely translate as, "Grab life with both hands and enjoy it!" **SERVES 6**

4 tablespoons unsalted butter, at room temperature
8 ounces thinly sliced Bayonne ham (or prosciutto)
4 large Idaho (baking) potatoes
Sea salt and freshly ground black pepper
Freshly grated nutmeg
2 garlic cloves, minced
2 cups crème fraîche
3½ ounces Emmental cheese, grated
2 black truffles, thinly sliced (optional)

Heat an *horno* or the oven to 350°F. Heavily butter a 2½- to 3-quart ovenproof casserole, including the underside of the lid, with the softened butter.

Starting in the center, line the casserole with overlapping slices of ham, allowing the excess to drape over the edges of the casserole. (You will fold these back over the potato filling before baking.)

Peel the potatoes and slice paper-thin on a mandoline. Do not wipe them or hold them in water—you want to retain the starch. Arrange one-third of the potatoes in an even layer in the bottom of the casserole. Season with salt, pepper, a light grating of nutmeg, and one-third of the minced garlic. Spread ⅔ cup of the crème fraîche over the potatoes and top with one-third of the grated cheese and, if using, one-third of the truffles. Continue making layers with the remaining ingredients in the same order. Fold the ham over the top to enclose the potatoes, and cover with the buttered lid.

Place in the oven and cook for 1½ hours. (If the casserole is very full, set it on a rimmed baking sheet in the oven in case it bubbles over.) When the gratin is done, the potatoes will be very soft, the cream will have bubbled up, and the ham will have crisped somewhat. Bring to the table and spoon out onto plates.

Creamy Potatoes with Leeks and Pancetta

I enjoy cooking in earthenware over a wood fire. Although I cannot give you a scientific reason, I am sure it has its own special way of heat transfer. I can never duplicate the results of risotto made in earthenware, for example, using metal cookware. I first learned to make a classic potato gratin, the loose inspiration for this dish, from Raymond Thuilier, with whom I worked when I was in my early twenties (he was eighty-nine!). He was an extraordinary man: not only a chef, but also a fine painter and the mayor of a town in Provence. Within three years of opening his restaurant, he had achieved three Michelin stars, the fastest anyone ever climbed that summit. This invention is dedicated to Chef Thuilier, who taught me that if you want to do something in your life, don't listen to people who tell you it's too late. **SERVES 6**

2 pounds Yukon Gold potatoes, scrubbed
2 tablespoons extra virgin olive oil
2 leeks, white and pale green parts only, minced
8 ounces smoked pancetta or lean bacon, diced
Coarse salt and freshly ground black pepper
1 cup crème fraîche
1 cup heavy cream
1 cup freshly grated Parmesan

Slice the potatoes about ½ inch thick on a mandoline.

Heat the olive oil in a heavy flameproof casserole over medium-low heat. Add the minced leeks and pancetta and sauté for about 8 minutes, until the leeks soften and start to turn golden and the pancetta has rendered most of its fat.

Add the potatoes, stir to combine, season to taste, cover, and continue cooking for about 15 minutes, until the potatoes are tender.

Mix the crème fraîche and heavy cream together and gently fold into the potatoes. Reduce the heat to a simmer and cook for several minutes more, until the cream thickens. Fold in the grated Parmesan and serve hot.

Smashed Potatoes

These addictive potatoes can be boiled and smashed in advance and then crisped just before serving. Flattening the potatoes results in a larger surface for the crunchy golden crust. **SERVES 4**

4 medium potatoes, about 5 ounces each, well scrubbed
2 tablespoons red wine vinegar
½ cup plus 2 tablespoons extra virgin olive oil
1 bay leaf
¼ teaspoon black peppercorns
Coarse salt

Place the potatoes, red wine vinegar, 2 tablespoons of the olive oil, the bay leaf, peppercorns, and salt to taste in a large saucepan, cover with cold water, and bring to a boil. Reduce the heat and cook at a gentle boil for 12 to 15 minutes, or until the potatoes are tender enough to be pierced through with a skewer. Drain in a colander; do not allow to cool, or the potatoes will break instead of smash.

Place a potato on one side of a clean dishcloth on a flat work surface and fold the cloth over to cover it. Using the palm of your hand, slowly and gently smash the potato inside the cloth. With a spatula, transfer to a plate. Repeat with the remaining potatoes.

Heat a *chapa* or a large cast-iron griddle or skillet over medium-low heat until a drop of water sizzles on the surface. Spoon a tablespoon of olive oil over each potato and place them oiled side down on the hot surface. Cook until they are crisp and golden on the bottom, about 5 minutes. Add the remaining ¼ cup oil to the skillet and slowly crisp the other side of the potatoes, about 5 minutes more. Serve immediately, sprinkled with coarse salt.

PICTURED ON PAGE V

Artichokes and Fingerling Potatoes a la Plancha

My dear friend Rose Gray, of London's famed River Café, was very fond of artichokes and almonds—two ingredients that are bitter when raw but, once cooked, have an earthy nuttiness. Here I decided to throw in my Patagonia wonder food . . . potatoes! Boiling the artichokes and potatoes and then caramelizing them on the *chapa* feels very Italian to me, as does the light vinaigrette of olive oil and lemon. **SERVES 4**

Coarse salt
4 lemons, 3 cut in half
4 large artichokes
12 fingerling potatoes, scrubbed
About ¼ cup extra virgin olive oil, plus more for drizzling
Freshly ground black pepper
1 bunch arugula, tough stems removed
⅓ cup toasted blanched whole almonds

Bring 2 inches of salted water to a boil in a large pot. Meanwhile, zest the whole lemon on a Microplane and reserve the zest. Cut the lemon in half and squeeze the juice into the pot. Toss in the squeezed halves.

For each artichoke, pull off most of the outside leaves, cut off most of the stem, and slice the remaining leaves off about two thirds of the way down to the base. With a sharp knife, trim off the tough green outside layer all around the base and stem. Rub the cut areas with the squeezed lemon halves and add to the pot with the trimmed artichokes. Reduce the heat to a gentle bubble and cook, covered, until the artichokes are tender when pierced through the bottom with a skewer, 15 minutes or so, depending on their size.

Meanwhile, place the potatoes in a pot of cold salted water and bring to a low boil over medium heat. Cook for about 10 minutes, or until they are tender enough to be easily pierced through with a skewer. Drain in a colander and let cool just enough to handle (if cooled completely, they will break instead of smash).

Put a potato on one half of a clean dishcloth on a work surface, fold the other half of the dishcloth over it, and, using the palm of your hand, slowly and gently smash the potato to flatten it. Transfer to a tray and repeat with the rest of the potatoes.

When the artichokes are done, drain them in a colander, stem side up so they drain thoroughly. Remove all the leaves. Using a teaspoon, scrape out the inedible chokes, then cut the artichokes into quarters. Pat them dry with paper towels, drizzle with a little olive oil to coat, and sprinkle with salt and pepper.

Heat a *chapa* or a large cast-iron griddle over medium heat. Scatter the arugula over a wide serving platter. Brush the *chapa* generously with olive oil, and when it shimmers, arrange the artichokes and lemon halves, cut side down, on the hot surface. Cook for about 2 minutes, until the artichokes are crisped and golden on the bottom. Turn and repeat until they are crisp and golden on all sides, then transfer to the platter. Remove the lemon halves when they are browned on the cut side and transfer to the platter.

As the artichokes are done, add the potatoes to the hot surface, adding more oil if necessary, and cook until the bottoms are crisped and golden, a minute or two. Turn and cook until crisped on the other side, then add to the platter.

Scatter the lemon zest and toasted almonds over the salad, season with salt and pepper, and serve immediately. At the table, everyone can squeeze the lemon halves over the top and drizzle with olive oil.

PICTURED ON PAGES 230–231

Artichokes and Fingerling Potatoes a la Plancha (page 229).

TRANCOSO, BRAZIL

How do you define tropical paradise? For me, it is Trancoso, a village on the coast of Brazil, a few hundred miles north of Rio, as pretty as any of Gauguin's tropical scenes.

It was the first place that the Portuguese explorer Pedro Alvares Cabral landed when he claimed Brazil for the king of Portugal. Not much else happened there for the next four hundred years, until a bunch of hippies rediscovered it in the 1970s. It was their idea of paradise too: a great beach, no cars, no malls, with fruits falling off the trees and fish jumping out of the river and ocean right into your frying pan. Vanina and I thought it sounded like just the place for us, so we booked a room in the only hotel in town and fell in love with Trancoso. Before we left, we told the hotelier that if a restaurant space became available, we would love to do something there. Two years later, I received a phone call about a small place—maybe fifty seats. No walls, just a roof and a place to cook over fires. In other words, a perfect spot for my brand of outdoor cooking and eating and hanging out. Now we spend two months there every winter. Our baby, Eloisa, is as happy there as a kitten with a ball of catnip.

The town—really just a village— is a cluster of ancient, or at least ancient-looking, cottages ranged around the *quadrado*, the rustic town green, with trees that throw the most seductive shade and grass that is tended only by grazing horses that keep it at just the right length. No cars. No screens in any windows, just wooden shutters, and shady porches for lolling around, reading a book, and listening to the breeze, the birds, the laughter of children at play. The huge tides from the ocean push for miles up the river, so if you are in the mood for a lazy float into the jungle, jump in and let the tide carry you upstream and, when it turns, return you to town. If you want to sunbathe, head for the beach, and if hunger should strike, make sure to raise your hand so that one of the many vendors can set up a brazier of hot coals and prepare some melted cheese on skewers. Fresh shrimp too. If this gets you thirsty, every beach has a bar, and every bartender makes ice-cold caipirinhas with the finest cachaça in the world. Or if vodka is your choice, then a caipiroska or two . . . or three.

Among the local fish, the vermilion snapper is as beautiful as its name and as delicious as it is beautiful. And the open-air market on Saturday! As you would expect in the tropics, there are pineapples and bananas, mangoes and papayas—the best I have ever tasted. If juice stains on your shirt are the price of such pleasure, I am ready to tie-dye my favorite dress shirt in mango nectar. Don't let me forget the beans. People don't, as a rule, get too excited at the mention of beans, but surely,

then, they have never had the freshly harvested beans that are a staple of the local diet here.

Finally, if you are a napper—which is the very definition of proper civilized living—you will find yourself among many aficionados of this low-impact sport. Of course, a nap is even more delicious with someone you love.

In the relative cool of the dawn—which is when I rise—I throw open the shutters as the first light touches the swirling mist rising off the trees and flowers. I sip a coffee and watch the late-night partygoers making their way home—some of them from my restaurant. My day is just starting.

DESSERTS

Burnt Peaches and Figs with Amaretto, Lemon Zest, and Mint

If you cook torn or sliced peaches in sugar on a hot *chapa,* they will caramelize quickly, with a slightly bitter edge, while the inside remains uncooked and sweet. I don't bother taking out the pits: I like the fruit served as rustically as possible. As a last step, I pour amaretto over the hot peaches and give them a final caramelization with more sugar. I use a salamander—kind of a hot branding iron—for this; it creates hissing, smoking steam as it sears the surface of the peaches. If you don't have a salamander, you can get much the same effect by sprinkling the sugar on the peaches and turning them sugared side down on the hot *chapa.* **SERVES 4**

4 ripe peaches
4 fresh figs
1 cup sugar
1 cup amaretto
Grated zest of 1 lemon
½ cup fresh mint leaves

Heat a *chapa* or a large cast-iron skillet over medium heat. Cut or tear the peaches in half, leaving the pits intact. Tear the figs in half. If using a salamander, place it in the fire to heat.

When the cooking surface is hot, spread half the sugar evenly over it. When it starts to melt, arrange the peaches and figs on it, skin side down. After several minutes, when the bottoms of the peaches are browned, carefully pour ¾ cup of the amaretto over the fruit, averting your face in case it flames up. Sprinkle with the remaining sugar. If using a salamander, brown the cut sides of the peaches for about 5 seconds each; otherwise, turn the peaches over to brown the cut sides. Pour the remaining ¼ cup of amaretto over the peaches.

Transfer the burnt fruit to a platter, sprinkle with the grated lemon zest, and scatter the mint leaves over all.

NOTE: Burnt sugar can be easily scraped off cast iron with a vinegar and water solution poured directly on the hot surface.

ALSO PICTURED ON PAGE 240

Grilled Bizcochuelo Strips with Amaretto and Burnt Shredded Quince

Bizcochuelo is a simple, very light cake. When it is sliced into strips, sprinkled with amaretto, dipped in sugar syrup, and grilled on the *parrilla,* it is striking to look at and delicious to eat. I like to serve it with Roasted Pineapple (page 254). Done on the grill, the pineapple comes out almost like a fruit confit (if you are cooking indoors, it turns out very well in the oven). I always dip the cake in the delicious caramelized syrup the pineapple has cooked in. If you skip the pineapple, use simple syrup. **SERVES 8**

FOR THE BIZCOCHUELO
Butter and flour for the pan
4 large eggs, at room temperature
¾ cup sugar
1 teaspoon fine salt
1 teaspoon vanilla extract
¾ cup cake flour, sifted
¼ cup amaretto

2 cups syrup from Roasted Pineapple (page 254)
    or Simple Syrup (recipe follows)
Vegetable oil
Burnt Shredded Quince (opposite), cut into slices
2 cups mascarpone cheese, Greek yogurt,
    or ice cream
Grated zest of 1 orange
Fresh mint leaves

To prepare the bizcochuelo, heat the oven to 350°F with a rack in the lower third. Butter and flour an 8-inch square cake pan. Line the bottom with a piece of parchment paper and butter and flour the parchment.

Break the eggs into the bowl of an electric mixer and add the sugar and salt. Beat with the whisk attachment at high speed until the mixture doubles in volume. Add the vanilla and continue beating until the mixture forms a ribbon when the beater is lifted. Remove the bowl from the mixer and, using a rubber spatula, gently but thoroughly fold in the sifted flour in 3 batches.

Pour the batter into the prepared pan. Bake for about 25 minutes, until the cake is golden brown on top and a skewer inserted in the center comes out clean. Let cool for about 10 minutes in the pan, then unmold onto a rack and cool completely.

When ready to serve, heat a charcoal grill or a large ridged cast-iron grill pan over high heat. Cut the bizcochuelo into quarters and cut each quarter into ½-inch-thick slices. Lay them out on a tray and sprinkle with the amaretto. Pour the syrup into a wide bowl and, using tongs, dip each strip quickly into the syrup and return to the tray; don't let them soak up too much syrup, or they will fall apart.

Brush the grill or pan with oil, lay the slices of cake on the grill (or in the pan), and grill, without disturbing them, for about 2 minutes, or until they are nicely marked. Turn and repeat on the other side. Transfer to a platter

To serve, place 4 bizcochuelo strips on each serving plate. Arrange some of the quince and a dollop of mascarpone or yogurt, or scoop of ice cream, beside them. Scatter the orange zest over the top and garnish with mint leaves.

Simple Syrup

MAKES ABOUT 1½ CUPS

1 cup sugar
1 cup water

Combine the sugar and water in a small saucepan. Bring to a boil, reduce the heat, and simmer for 3 minutes, stirring occasionally, until the sugar is completely dissolved. The syrup will keep for several weeks tightly covered in the refrigerator.

Burnt Shredded Quince

In Argentina, and throughout much of the Hispanic world, quince is made into blocks of paste, called *membrillo*, often eaten with cream cheese as an appetizer or dessert. For this simple recipe, shredded quince is sprinkled with sugar and cooked on a *chapa*. Usually quince takes a very long time to cook. I particularly like this method because the quince cooks quickly. The sugar caramelizes and the sugar and butter soften the flavors and balance the fruit's natural tartness. Serve over ice cream or as a garnish for poached fruits. **MAKES ABOUT 1½ CUPS**

1 quince
2 tablespoons unsalted butter
¼ cup sugar

Heat a *chapa* or a cast-iron griddle over high heat. Meanwhile, peel the quince and shred it on a box grater, avoiding the seedy core.

When the *chapa* is hot enough for a drop of water to sizzle on the surface, rub the butter over it and spread the shredded quince on top. Sprinkle the sugar evenly over the quince, and don't disturb for at least 2 minutes, until nicely browned on the bottom. Turn and repeat on the other side. Serve hot or warm.

Textiles

I collect old textiles by the hundreds. Ancient batik from Indonesia, old indigo-dyed fabrics from Africa, Alsatian squared linens, antique damask from Persia, vicuña wools from the Andes, hand-sewn saris from India, Aubusson rugs from France, and needlepoint from England are all part of my family. They have all been on my TV shoots, in a tent in the snow, on a grill day at the beach, or used as tablecloths on my farm in the hills of Uruguay. They give comfort and warmth on the sofas of my log cabin on a remote island in Patagonia, hang from the roof of my restaurant in Trancoso in the north of Brazil, and add color to my bathroom in Buenos Aires (which has three sofas). Each is a memory of a time and a place. I catch a glimpse of a tiny part of one in a stack and am taken back, for example, to Paris in the 80s when I bought it even though I then had barely enough money left to pay my hotel bill.

Pionono with Dulce de Leche and Strawberries

Originally a pastry from Spain, in Argentina, *pionono* is a sponge cake rolled up around either a sweet or a savory filling. Here it is stuffed with fresh strawberries and dulce de leche. The sugars crisp and slightly burn on the grill, and I think that by now, you know I love char on almost anything. **SERVES 8**

FOR THE PASTRY
Butter and flour for the pan
6 large eggs
⅓ cup sugar
1 teaspoon fine salt
1 teaspoon vanilla extract
½ cup cake flour, sifted twice

FOR THE FILLING
1 pound dulce de leche, preferably La Salamandra
1 pint strawberries, hulled
Vegetable oil

To prepare the cake, heat an *horno* or the oven to 375°F, with a rack in the lower third. Butter a 12-by-16-by-¾-inch rimmed baking sheet, line it with parchment paper, and butter and flour the paper. Set aside.

Break the eggs into the bowl of an electric mixer and add the sugar, salt, and vanilla. Beat with the whisk attachment at high speed for 5 to 10 minutes, until the mixture is very thick and light and forms a ribbon when the beater is lifted. With a rubber spatula, fold in the sifted flour, taking care to break up any lumps.

Pour the batter into the prepared pan and spread it evenly. Bake for 10 minutes, or until the cake is firm to the touch and is beginning to pull away from the sides of the pan. Lay another piece of parchment on top of the cake and invert it onto the paper. Cover with a damp kitchen towel and let cool completely.

Have a bowl of hot water at hand. Spoon the dulce de leche onto the cooled cake and spread it evenly with a spatula until the surface is covered, leaving a ¼-inch border. You may need to dip the spatula in the hot water at intervals if the dulce de leche gets too sticky.

If the strawberries are large, halve or quarter them. Scatter them evenly over the dulce de leche. Using the parchment to help you, roll up the cake from a short end as you would a jelly roll. If the cake sticks, sprinkle some hot water onto the back of the parchment paper to help release the cake. Turn the roll seam side down and cut it into 8 slices.

Heat a charcoal grill or a large ridged cast-iron grill pan over medium-high heat. Brush the grill or pan generously with vegetable oil. Arrange the slices of *pionono* on the hot surface, spaced well apart (cook in batches if necessary), and grill for about a minute, until nicely marked on the bottom. Using a wide sharp-edged spatula, transfer the grilled *pionono* to individual dessert plates and serve immediately.

Pears with Malbec, Cream, and Berries

Fruit, cream, and wine—these are three food groups I could eat every day. There is no place on earth that produces more luscious berries than the mountain valleys and hillsides of Patagonia. The days are long and very sunny and the nights are cold: perfect conditions for berries. Many of these berries aren't cultivated—in fact, some I haven't seen anywhere else in the world. The deep purple, almost black, *calafate* and *sauco* of the Andes have delighted me on many a mountain hike. Likewise, the orchards of the valley of the Rio Negro, because of that same cycle of long hot days and cold nights, yield the most wonderful pears. Malbec grapes, originally vinted in France for the hearty black wine of Cahors, express a bit more elegance in the vineyards of our wine country in Mendoza. It still makes for a full-bodied, intensely fruity wine that reduces to a silky syrup. **SERVES 4**

4 large ripe pears
28 whole cloves
2 bottles (750 ml each) Malbec
1 cup sugar, or more to taste
1 cup very cold heavy cream
2 cups berries, such as raspberries, blueberries, and blackberries

Stud the pears with 7 cloves each. Combine the wine and sugar in a large saucepan, add the pears, and bring to a gentle simmer over low heat. Cook for about 1 hour, until the pears are tender all the way through; they should be soft enough to eat with a spoon but not falling apart. Remove from the poaching liquid and set them aside.

Raise the heat to medium and reduce the wine to a syrup, tasting about halfway through. The flavor will be very intense; add more sugar if it's too tart.

Whip the cream until soft peaks form. Arrange the pears on serving plates and slash them open. Fill with the whipped cream, garnish with the berries, and drizzle the syrup over all.

Broiled Sabayon with Berries

In my early childhood, when we lived on the shores of Lake Nahuel Huapi, we had a wonderful garden on the property and every berry you could imagine. There is a songbird there called a *sorcal,* which loves our wild berries as much as I do. My brother, Carlos, and I would go out berry picking in the afternoon and it was always a competition to get them before the sorcal did. My grandmother, Tata, would make a great *sambayon* (sabayon) to serve with them and, like every chef, I often measure traditional recipes against those of my grandmother.

Do not let the egg yolks get too warm, or they will scramble. You can lift the bowl and continue beating off the heat if the sabayon seems to be thickening too quickly. **SERVES 4**

6 large egg yolks, at room temperature
6 tablespoons sugar
3 tablespoons port
1 tablespoon Armagnac
1 pint fresh berries, one kind or a mix
1 tablespoon chopped toasted almonds
1 tablespoon chopped toasted hazelnuts
1 tablespoon chopped toasted walnuts

Preheat the broiler. Place the egg yolks and sugar in a medium stainless steel bowl, set over a saucepan of barely simmering water, and, with an electric mixer, beat until very light and foamy and beginning to thicken.

Spread the sabayon in a large gratin dish or shallow baking dish and set the berries into it, spacing them about an inch apart. Set under the broiler for a minute or two, rotating the dish if necessary to brown the sabayon evenly and watching carefully so it does not burn. Sprinkle the toasted nuts over the top and bring immediately to the table.

PICTURED ON PAGE 252

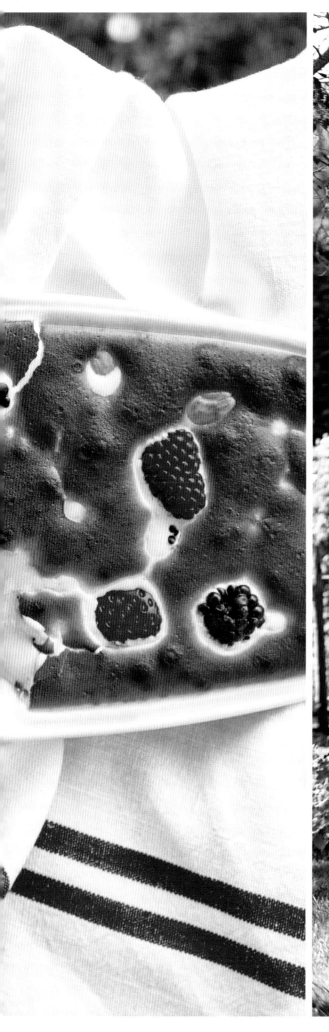

Sabayon Ice Cream with Roasted Pineapple and Gooseberry Jelly

When I was a boy, I was on the thin side, and my parents would feed me *sambayon* every day in the hope that I would put on weight. This is the opposite of the problem many of us face as adults. Still, you never outgrow your childhood favorites, or at least I never did, so whenever I am looking for a dessert that will satisfy both my grown-up tastes and my childhood memories, this is the one. It makes for a fine showcase for slow-roasted pineapple—a trick I picked up in Brazil. **SERVES 6**

FOR THE ICE CREAM
8 large egg yolks
½ cup sugar
2 tablespoons port
2 cups very cold heavy cream

FOR THE ROASTED PINEAPPLE
2 cups water
2 cups sugar
1 ripe, juicy pineapple

1 cup gooseberry jelly

Place the egg yolks and sugar in a large stainless steel bowl, set over a saucepan of barely simmering water, and beat with an electric mixer until very light and creamy and beginning to thicken. Watch the temperature of the mixture carefully, and scrape it from the bottom and sides of the bowl often so it does not overheat and scramble. Add the port and continue beating until the sabayon is foamy and tripled in volume. Remove from the heat and cool to room temperature.

Whip the cream just until it forms stiff peaks, and fold it gently but thoroughly into the cooked custard. Refrigerate until chilled.

Pour the mixture into an ice cream machine and freeze according to the manufacturer's instructions. Transfer to a freezer container and freeze overnight.

To make the roasted pineapple: If cooking outdoors, heat a charcoal grill over medium heat. If cooking indoors, heat the oven to 375°F.

Pour the water into a saucepan, add the sugar, and heat over medium heat, stirring occasionally, until the sugar dissolves. Pour into a deep roasting pan just large enough to hold the pineapple.

Slice off the bottom and top of the pineapple. Remove the skin and trim out the eyes. Lay the pineapple in the syrup and turn to soak all sides. If cooking outdoors, grill the pineapple slowly, turning to brown all sides. Occasionally dunk it in the syrup to baste, using tongs to turn it over in the syrup. The pineapple should be tender in about 1 hour. If cooking indoors, lay the pineapple on its side in a roasting pan and bake until it is tender all the way through and very juicy but still holds its shape, about 1 hour. Every 15 minutes, take the pineapple out, roll it in the syrup to baste, and return to the pan, rotating the pan.

Transfer the pineapple to a cutting board and let rest for 5 minutes. (Reserve the syrup for another use, such as the Grilled Bizcochuelo Strips on page 244.)

Melt the gooseberry jelly in a saucepan over medium heat. With a long serrated knife, cut the pineapple into ¾-inch-thick slices. Arrange on individual dessert plates with a scoop of the ice cream, and drizzle with the melted gooseberry jelly.

VARIATION:
Sabayon Ice Cream with Roasted Grapes
Prepare the ice cream base and start freezing it according to the manufacturer's instructions. When the ice cream is almost frozen, add ½ cup stemmed Roasted Grapes (page 282), while the motor is running, and proceed as directed.

PRECEDING: Broiled Sabayon with Berries (page 251).

Pressed Pears and Plums in Red Wine with Rosemary (page 258). I pressed these pears under a 60-pound paving stone, but you will do just as well by stacking some cast-iron skillets, Dutch ovens, or bricks.

Pressed Pears and Plums in Red Wine with Rosemary

Pressing any fruit concentrates its flavor. If you use enough weight, the fruit becomes so dense that when you serve it, you eat the most heavenly pudding. I often add a touch of rosemary: Its savoriness helps to focus the broad sweet fruit flavor.

You can vary the amount of sugar depending on the sweetness of the fruit. **SERVES 8**

6 ripe pears
6 large ripe plums
2 cups sugar, or to taste
2 to 3 bottles (750 ml each) light red wine, such as Uruguayan Tannat
A large bunch of rosemary
2 lemons
Ice cream or whipped cream

Heat an *horno* or the oven to 350°F.

Arrange the pears, on their sides, and plums in a single layer in a large deep roasting pan. Pour the sugar and 2 bottles of the wine over the fruit, and scatter the rosemary branches on top. Wrap a slightly smaller roasting pan in foil to protect it and place it on top of the sugared fruit. Weight this pan with as many heavy bricks or cast-iron skillets as will fit (and that you are able to lift).

Move the whole thing into the oven and bake for about 2 hours, checking the wine level every 30 minutes and adding more wine as it evaporates; check more frequently during the second hour to make sure the fruit does not burn. You want to end up with flattened pears and plums and a syrupy red wine sauce.

Transfer the fruit and syrup to a wide shallow serving platter. Grate the zest of the lemons over the fruit, and serve with ice cream or whipped cream.

PICTURED ON PAGES 256–257

Dulce de Leche Ice Cream

One of the most extravagantly sweet and caloric recipes, dulce de leche ice cream is the single most popular dessert in all of my restaurants. Freezing lightens the overwhelmingly sweet effect of the dulce de leche. Serve with any burnt (charred) fruit, such as bananas or strawberries. If you keep going back for more, as we Argentines do, wear loose-fitting trousers! **MAKES ABOUT 1 QUART**

2 cups whole milk
1 pound dulce de leche, preferably La Salamandra
½ cup heavy cream

Pour the milk into a heavy saucepan, add the dulce de leche, and cook over medium heat, stirring constantly with a wooden spoon or a wire whisk, until the dulce de leche is completely melted and blended with the milk; the mixture should be a dark caramel color and perfectly smooth. Transfer to a stainless steel bowl and set into a larger bowl of ice water to cool.

Whisk the heavy cream into the dulce de leche mixture to blend and refrigerate until chilled.

Pour the ice cream base into an ice cream machine and freeze according to the manufacturer's instructions. Transfer to a freezer container and freeze until firm before serving.

Chocolate Torta del Lago with Nuts and Dulce de Leche

This cake is delicious and extremely rich—a small slice goes a long way. Sometimes I use only hazelnuts, but a combination of nuts, such as walnuts and almonds, works well too. Dusting the nuts lightly with flour before adding them to the batter keeps them from sinking to the bottom. **SERVES 8**

Butter and flour for the pan
12 ounces bittersweet chocolate (70% cacao), chopped
¾ pound (3 sticks) unsalted butter, cut into pieces
6 large eggs, separated
6 tablespoons sugar
½ cup sifted cake flour, plus extra for dusting
5 ounces (1 cup) hazelnuts or other nuts, or a mix, coarsely chopped
1 pound dulce de leche, preferably La Salamandra

Heat an *horno* or the oven to 350°F, with a rack in the center. Butter and flour an 8-inch springform pan. Cut a circle of parchment paper to fit the pan and line the bottom with it. Butter and flour the parchment.

Place the chocolate and butter in a metal bowl or the top of a double boiler and set over hot, but not simmering, water; do not let the bottom of the bowl touch the water. Melt the chocolate and butter together slowly, stirring every few minutes. Do not overheat, or the chocolate will seize (become lumpy). Remove from the heat and cool to tepid.

Using an electric mixer, beat the egg yolks with the sugar in a large bowl until the mixture forms a ribbon when the beaters are lifted. Gradually but thoroughly mix in the flour. Fold in 1½ cups of the melted chocolate mixture, making sure it is thoroughly combined. Dust the nuts lightly with a little flour and fold them in too.

Mix half the dulce de leche into the remaining chocolate mixture and set it aside for the glaze.

Using clean beaters, beat the egg whites in a large bowl until they are stiff but not dry. Gently but thoroughly fold them into the batter.

Pour the batter into the prepared pan and set it on a baking sheet. Bake for about 35 minutes, or until a bamboo skewer inserted in the center of the cake comes out clean. Let the cake cool for about 15 minutes before removing the sides of the pan, then cool completely on a rack.

Slice the cake horizontally into 3 layers. Put the first layer on a serving plate and spread it with half the remaining dulce de leche. Set the second layer on top and spread with the rest of the dulce de leche. Set the top layer on top, smooth side up.

Gently heat the chocolate–dulce de leche mixture over hot water until it is of pouring consistency. Pour it evenly over the top of the cake, letting it drip down the sides, then use a spatula to spread the glaze evenly over the sides. Refrigerate the cake to set the glaze before serving.

PICTURED ON PAGES 260–261

Making Chocolate Torta del Lago with Nuts and Dulce de Leche
(page 259) for my grade-school teacher Edith Jones.

COUNTRY BREADS

Tarta de Picho

My Aunt Mecha had an English-style teashop in Montevideo in the 1960s called The Teapot. She served just one kind of tea, a special blend of half Lapsang souchong and half Earl Grey, along with a few pastries and scones. The shop was open only from 4 until 7 p.m., and it was always packed. This recipe has been closely guarded by my grandmother and then my mother, Picho, until now. I hope it becomes a family tradition for you too. **SERVES 6**

4 cups self-rising flour
1 teaspoon baking powder
2 large eggs
¾ cup olive oil, plus more for brushing
1 cup whole milk
8 ounces sliced boiled ham
8 ounces cuartirolo or fresh mozzarella cheese, sliced ¼ inch thick
1 tablespoon sugar

Combine the flour and baking powder in a large bowl. Beat one of the eggs, then make a well in the flour and, using a fork, quickly mix in the beaten egg, olive oil, and milk, pulling it all together into a soft dough. Turn it out onto a floured board and knead it together for a minute or two. Shape it into a disk, wrap in plastic wrap, and chill for 1 hour.

Heat an *horno* or the oven to 375°F.

Divide the dough in half. Brush a 9½-inch springform pan with olive oil and lightly press half the dough into it with your fingers. Cover the dough with the slices of ham, and cover them with the cheese. Press the other half of the dough out into a circle the same size as the pan and set it on top of the cheese, pressing the edges together lightly to seal them.

Beat the second egg with 1 teaspoon water and brush this egg wash over the pastry. Sprinkle with the sugar. Bake for about 25 minutes, until the tarta is golden brown on top and a skewer inserted in the center comes out clean. Cool for several minutes, then remove the sides of the pan and serve the tarta warm, sliced into wedges.

Tarta of Cuartirolo Cheese and Red Grapes

Cream cheese and jelly is a favorite of kids in North America, and this recipe marries my Aunt Mecha's tarta with an Argentinean version of that combination.

The dough is quite soft, so chill it well and work quickly. **SERVES 6**

2 tablespoons extra virgin olive oil
Tarta de Picho dough (at left), well chilled
8 ounces seedless red or black grapes
8 ounces cuartirolo or fresh mozzarella cheese, sliced about ¼ inch thick
1 large egg plus 1 large egg yolk, lightly beaten
2 tablespoons sugar

Heat an *horno* or the oven to 375°F. Oil a medium baking sheet with the olive oil.

Divide the dough in half. Set half the dough in the center of the baking sheet and, using your fingers, press it out into a rough circle ½ to ¾ inch thick and 9 inches in diameter. Arrange the grapes evenly over it, crushing them slightly with your fingers as you set them in the dough. Layer the cheese evenly over the grapes.

Set the other half of the dough on a sheet of waxed paper and press it out into a circle slightly larger than the first one. Slide a pastry scraper or wide spatula under it, lift it up, and drape it over the cheese and grapes. Crimp the edges with a fork to seal and brush with the beaten egg to glaze. Sprinkle with half the sugar.

Bake the tarta for about 25 minutes, until nicely browned on top. Sprinkle with the remaining sugar, slice into wedges, and serve warm.

Pan de Molde

This is our favorite breakfast in Garzón, a hearty no-knead dark loaf made with a semiliquid batter. *Molde* refers to the fact that it's baked in a loaf pan. It is wonderful for toast. I find that it is a very noble dough that generously accepts all kinds of dried fruits and nuts. Thanks to Pilar Soria for this recipe. For years, she has kept my businesses together and made sure that things go right . . . when I cooperate. She has been my rock. **MAKES 1 LOAF**

One ¼-ounce package active dry yeast
2 tablespoons honey
2 cups warm water (100° to 110°F)
2¼ cups whole wheat flour
1 cup plus 3 tablespoons all-purpose flour,
**   plus more for the pan**
1 tablespoon coarse salt
¾ cup walnuts, chopped
⅓ cup raisins
Butter for the pan

Combine the yeast, honey, and ¼ cup of the warm water in a small bowl and let stand until foamy.

Combine the flours and salt in the bowl of a heavy-duty mixer fitted with the paddle attachment. Add the nuts and raisins and mix to coat them, then mix in the yeast mixture. With the mixer on medium speed, gradually add the remaining 1¾ cups water, mixing until a batter-like dough forms. Scrape into a large floured bowl and let rise in a warm place until doubled in volume, about 2 hours.

Preheat an *horno* or the oven to 350°F. Butter and flour an 8½-by-4½-by-2½-inch loaf pan.

Stir down the dough and scrape it into the prepared pan. Bake for about 55 minutes, or until the top is crusted and brown and a bamboo skewer inserted in the center comes out clean. The bottom should sound hollow when tapped. Let cool slightly in the pan, then turn out and cool completely on a rack before slicing.

Sopa Paraguaya

Although *sopa* means soup, this Paraguayan favorite is not a soup at all, but a corn bread layered with onions and fresh cheese. As the layers bake, they blend into a kind of lasagna. **SERVES 8**

2 tablespoons extra virgin olive oil
1¼ cups stone-ground yellow cornmeal
3 onions, finely chopped
1½ cups whole milk
3 large eggs, lightly beaten
1 teaspoon coarse salt
½ teaspoon freshly ground black pepper
1 teaspoon crushed red pepper flakes, or to taste
1¼ cups finely diced fresh mozzarella

Heat an *horno* or the oven to 375°F, with a rack in the lower third. Brush a 9-by-5-by-3-inch loaf pan well with 1 tablespoon of the olive oil and coat with ¼ cup of the cornmeal.

Heat the remaining 1 tablespoon olive oil in a large skillet over low heat. Add the onions and sauté until tender and translucent; do not let them brown. Set aside to cool to room temperature.

In a medium bowl, mix together the milk, beaten eggs, salt, pepper, red pepper flakes, and cooled onions.

Sprinkle one-third of the remaining cornmeal evenly over the bottom of the pan. Scatter one-third of the mozzarella evenly over it. Ladle one-third of the milk, egg, and onion mixture over the cheese. Repeat two more times. The mixture will look quite wet.

Set the pan on a baking sheet and bake for about 1 hour, until puffed and golden brown and quite fluffy; do not let it get too firm, or it will be dry. Cool in the pan on a rack.

Run a metal spatula around the sides of the pan to loosen the *sopa,* place a platter or tray over the top, and invert to unmold.

Black Bread with Nuts

It's fun to have special recipes for special times and places. This is a bread that I only make when I am on The Island. Often I will bring along some hazelnuts, walnuts, and chestnuts gathered in the forests of Mendoza just for this bread. It is a dense, black health loaf that keeps for weeks. Slice it very thin for the most beautiful toast. **MAKES 1 LOAF**

One ¼-ounce package active dry yeast

1½ teaspoons sugar

2⅓ cups warm water (100° to 110°F)

1½ cups whole wheat flour

1½ cups unprocessed miller's wheat bran
   (available from Bob's Red Mill)

1½ cups raw wheat germ

1 tablespoon coarse salt

2 cups coarsely chopped toasted nuts, such as
   hazelnuts and/or walnuts

All-purpose flour for dusting

Extra virgin olive oil for the pan

Combine the yeast, sugar, and ⅓ cup of the warm water in a small bowl and let stand for about 10 minutes, until foamy.

Combine the flour, bran, wheat germ, and salt in the bowl of a heavy-duty mixer fitted with the paddle attachment and mix on medium speed. Add the yeast mixture and the remaining 2 cups warm water and, mix until a wet, batter-like dough forms. Dust the nuts with a little all-purpose flour and, with the motor running, add them to the flour mixture and mix until well combined. Scrape into a floured bowl and set in a warm place to rise until doubled in size, about 2 hours.

Heat an *horno* or the oven to 350°F. Oil an 8½-by-4½-by-2½-inch loaf pan and dust it with flour.

Stir down the dough and scrape it into the pan—it will come almost to the top. Bang the pan on the counter a few times to get rid of any air bubbles. Bake for about 55 minutes, or until the top is brown and crusty and a bamboo skewer inserted in the center comes out clean. The bottom should sound hollow when tapped. Cool slightly, then unmold and let cool completely on a rack before slicing.

Chapa Bread

Our romantic, rough-and-tumble gauchos would split open the bread and toss in a slice of meat straight from the *parrilla*. **MAKES 12 SMALL BREADS**

One ¼-ounce package active dry yeast
1 tablespoon sugar
¼ cup warm water (100° to 110°F)
3 cups sifted all-purpose flour, plus more for
   dusting
1 tablespoon coarse salt
1 cup warm milk (100° to 110°F)

Combine the yeast, sugar, and warm water in a small bowl and let stand for about 10 minutes, until foamy.

Whisk together the flour and salt in a large bowl. Make a well in the center and stir in the yeast mixture. Gradually stir in the warm milk, then bring it all together with your hands into a soft dough.

Flour a work surface, turn the dough out, and knead for about 5 minutes, until smooth. Shape into a ball, put in a floured bowl, and let rise, covered with plastic wrap and a damp cloth, in a warm place for about 2 hours, until doubled in size.

Turn the dough out onto a floured surface and roll it under your palms into a cylinder about 2 inches thick and 14 inches long. Cut into 12 disks. Stretch each disk out with your fingers until about ½ inch thick and lay the disks on a floured baking sheet spaced well apart. Cover with a damp cloth and let rise a second time until puffy, about 30 minutes.

Heat a *chapa* or a cast-iron griddle over medium-low heat. Cook the breads, in batches if necessary, for about 5 minutes on each side, until puffed and lightly browned.

To serve, split open with a knife. Fill with desired sandwich ingredients.

Scones from The Teapot

These very crumbly scones must be eaten immediately for the most tender consistency. They toughen as they sit. Almost all of the mixing should be done with a fork; you barely touch the dough with your hands. When I was a schoolboy in Bariloche, every day when I got home from my studies (or at least I was supposed to be studying), I would have some of these with butter and jam. The hot scones would melt the butter. A heavenly memory!
MAKES 16 SCONES

Vegetable oil for the baking sheet
4 cups sifted self-rising flour
4 tablespoons cold unsalted butter
2 large eggs
1 cup milk
Grated zest of 1 lemon
Pinch of fine salt
2 tablespoons sugar

Heat an *horno* or the oven to 400°F. Oil a large baking sheet.

Put the flour in a bowl and cut the butter into it with two forks or a pastry blender.

Break one egg into a bowl and lightly beat in the milk, lemon zest, and salt. Make a well in the center of the flour mixture and pour in the egg mixture. Working quickly, bring it all together with a fork into a soft, shaggy dough; do not overwork.

Turn out the dough and shape it into a thick roll about 16 inches long. Cut it into sixteen 1-inch pieces and arrange them about 1 inch apart on the baking sheet. Beat the second egg and brush it over the scones to glaze them. Sprinkle with the sugar.

Bake for about 15 minutes, or until the scones are golden, rotating the pan halfway through. Serve immediately.

"THE ISLAND,"
PATAGONIA

There are many islands in the world, but, for me, there is only one place that is *The* Island. It is in a remote lake in Patagonia, a hundred miles down a dirt road and then an hour by boat across the lake. It is surrounded by the Valdivian Forest—an actual alpine rain forest on the slope of the Andes just over the mountains from Chile. Through all the changes in my life, it has been my one constant, my "true north"—although it is actually to the south. It is where I go to rest, to think, to be alone with family and special friends. The only other creatures are the waterbirds, brook trout, huge Andean condors, deer, and mountain lions. There are wild mushrooms by the basketful.

I built the main cabin with my late friend Marcial and my brother, Carlos, who shares my affection for the wild heart of Patagonia. The cabin sits in the lee of the winds coming off the Andes and the storms that blow in from the west. Twenty years ago, I thought that was perfect, but now I want to see those storms and feel them as they roll in, so I built my own private cabin on The Island's other side, with a perfect view of the incoming tempests.

I always insist on at least ten days on The Island for me and for my guests. The first three days, you are still filled with the concerns of the outside world, but then the quiet and the solitude and the immensity of nature take over and you move to a different clock, the timeless metronome of Patagonia. No phones, no Internet. You get to know people in a new way. It is a very intimate situation, so I have learned to choose my guests well. Everybody reveals themselves. Are they enjoying it or not? Are they scared? Do they feel that the place is too remote? Or have they shed the skin of civilization and slipped into the primeval wilderness?

The house is ruled by fire: a woodstove inside and a *chapa*, a *parrilla*, and an *horno* in a hut by the lakefront. My kitchen is quite basic and rough, but I have very good pots and pans, lots of cast iron, of course. I bake bread every two days and make fresh pasta as the spirit strikes me, which is often. I have a chocolate cake that I only make when I am on The Island. There is fresh brook trout whenever you want it; in half an hour, you can catch enough one- to two-pound trout to feed everyone for lunch and dinner. And I carry in beautiful meat: big briskets, rib roasts, steaks.

At nearly 4,000 feet, the climate, especially in winter, is quite harsh, but even when the snow is piled to the eaves of the cabin and we have to dig our way in, there is no place I would rather be. Because it is so remote and the winters so intense, I

had assumed that the native peoples never visited my island. I could imagine no reason for them to venture from the lakeshore, if indeed they had ever made it to that supremely isolated spot. But last year I found a sharpening stone, unmistakably the work of the Mapuches, who still live throughout Patagonia. I envision them here five thousand years ago, digging a *curanto* pit to cook a deer. And afterward, perhaps having a dessert of wild berries gathered in the forest.

BASICS

Chilled Flavored Olive Oil

I had a bottle of chimichurri in my refrigerator and it struck me that when the olive oil congealed, it looked like butter. Then I thought, why not add different herbs or other ingredients to olive oil, chill it, and serve it as a condiment with all kinds of food? In the same way that you might offer a choice of mustard or ketchup, I now put a selection of oils on the table with a roast or a fish and let my guests choose. I love it when the chilled oil melts just like a pat of butter and gives you a fresh, delicate flavor. I use parsley, thyme, oregano, chives, and rosemary, each in its own container.

It is critical that you chill flavored olive oil. I wish I could say chilling oil until it becomes solid was an inspiration, but in fact it was simply what happened whenever I returned to The Island; my chimichurri and my plain olive oil would turn solid in the cold nights. The cold oil reminded me so much of maître d'hôtel butter that I decided to use it like butter.
MAKES ABOUT 1 CUP

**1 cup packed fresh herb leaves—one herb only or
    a combination of herbs**
1 cup extra virgin olive oil

Wash the herbs and pat thoroughly dry with a kitchen towel. Lay a dry towel out on a baking sheet and spread the herb(s) out to air-dry. When they are completely dry, chop and stir into the olive oil.

Refrigerate in a tightly covered jar until ready to use. To keep for longer than a few days, store in small portions in the freezer.

Pimentón Oil

As a variation on the chilled herb oils, I like the peppery effect of pimentón as a flavoring, smoked or unsmoked, depending on the dish. The optional garlic adds a little kick. **MAKES 1 CUP**

**2 tablespoons pimentón (Spanish paprika),
    smoked or unsmoked**
1 cup extra virgin olive oil
1 teaspoon minced garlic (optional)

Put the pimentón in a bowl and stir in the olive oil. Add the garlic if desired. Let stand for 20 minutes, then strain.

Refrigerate in a tightly covered jar until ready to use. To keep for longer than a few days, store in small portions in the freezer.

Roasted Grapes on the Vine

This recipe was inspired by a schiacciata I had in Tuscany, a bread studded with grapes that caramelize as the bread is baked and are both burnt and sweet at the same time. I had completely forgotten about those grapes until one day last summer when Donna Gelb and I visited the vineyard of my friend Alejandro Bulgheroni, near Garzón. When I tasted his grapes, which were overripe, I immediately thought of that schiacciata. All I did here was to get rid of the bread part and keep the grapes. And ever since, I have been playing with adding roasted grapes to recipes—as a garnish for meat (see the Pork Loin Chops on page 134), or as a topping for desserts (see the Sabayon Ice Cream on page 254). **SERVES 4**

1 pound small red, white, or champagne grapes, in small bunches
¼ to ½ cup packed light brown sugar, depending on the sweetness of the grapes

Heat an *horno* or the oven to 475°F, with a rack in the lower third.

Pat the grapes dry and arrange them on a baking sheet. Sprinkle the sugar evenly over them and roast for about 15 minutes, until the grapes are nicely browned but still juicy. If they are not browned, pop them under the broiler for 3 minutes. Serve.

Toasted Nuts

I often use combinations of toasted nuts, sometimes adding a spoonful of the chopped nuts to a stew for texture or using them as a crunchy topping for poached fruit or ice cream or the base of a salsa. They keep well in an airtight jar. **MAKES 2 CUPS**

½ **cup shelled pistachios**
½ **cup unblanched whole almonds**
½ **cup walnuts**
½ **cup hazelnuts**

Heat the oven to 350°F.

Spread all the nuts out on a large baking sheet, keeping the hazelnuts separate. Toast in the oven for about 10 minutes, rotating the pan occasionally if they are browning unevenly. When they are golden brown and fragrant, remove from the oven. Transfer the pistachios, almonds, and walnuts to another baking sheet to cool. Wrap the hot hazelnuts in a clean dish towel and let steam for a minute or two, then briskly rub off most of the skins with the towel. Let cool completely.

Place all the cooled nuts in a food processor and pulse several times, until finely chopped. Do not overprocess, or they will become pasty. Store in a tightly sealed jar.

Toasted Nut Salsa

In the 1990s, I exchanged some staff with London's River Café when they were installing a wood oven like the one I had in Uruguay. At that time, they were making something like this salsa. I thought that it had the depth, yet lightness, to add layers of flavor to grilled fish. **MAKES ABOUT 1¼ CUPS**

2 **tablespoons pimentón dulce**
   (sweet Spanish paprika)
2 **tablespoons sherry vinegar**
6 **tablespoons extra virgin olive oil**
¾ **cup chopped Toasted Nuts (at left)**
Coarse salt
Cayenne pepper

Whisk the pimentón into the sherry vinegar in a small bowl. Gradually whisk in the olive oil. Stir in the chopped nuts and season with salt and cayenne pepper to taste. The salsa is best served the same day it's made.

Salsa Llajua

This sweet, piquant, spicy all-purpose salsa is a favorite in the province of Jujuy. I first tasted it in a *huacho locro,* which is a traditional one-pot stew of corn, vegetables, and meat. *Huacho* is a lovely word in the Indian tongue; it means something like orphan, as in a goat that has lost its mother. And *llajua*, in the Indian tongue, means "spicy"—and I like it that way, especially with eggs. **MAKES ABOUT 1 CUP**

1 large ripe red or yellow tomato
½ teaspoon sugar
½ teaspoon coarse salt
1 tablespoon red wine vinegar
1 hot chile pepper, seeded and finely chopped
2 tablespoons extra virgin olive oil
Freshly ground black pepper
Crushed red pepper flakes (optional)

Using the coarse side of a box grater, grate the tomato, including the skin, into a bowl. Add the sugar, salt, vinegar, half the chile pepper, the olive oil, and black pepper to taste. Mix well, taste it, and wait 5 seconds. If it is not hot enough for your liking, add more of the chile and/or red pepper flakes until it is.

Salsa Provenzal

After chimichurri, this simple fresh sauce is the most popular condiment in Argentina. I've been told it is named for Provence because these are favorite ingredients in that sun-splashed part of France. **MAKES ABOUT 1 CUP**

½ cup packed minced fresh flat-leaf parsley
1 teaspoon minced garlic
½ cup extra virgin olive oil
Coarse salt and freshly ground black pepper

Combine the minced parsley and garlic in a small bowl. Slowly add the olive oil, whisking to combine. Season to taste with salt and pepper.

Salsa Criolla

Traditionally served with roast meat as an alternative to chimichurri, this light, colorful salsa is also great with eggs. **MAKES ABOUT 2 CUPS**

1 large red bell pepper
1 large yellow bell pepper
1 red onion, minced
¼ cup red wine vinegar
Coarse salt and freshly ground black pepper
½ cup extra virgin olive oil, or more as needed

Cut the peppers lengthwise in half and remove the stems and seeds. With a very sharp knife, remove all the white ribs. Slice the peppers into very fine strips, then mince very fine. Place in a small mixing bowl.

Add the minced onion to the peppers and mix well. Stir in the red wine vinegar and season with salt and pepper. Stir in the olive oil to combine. There should be enough to cover the onion and peppers; add more if necessary. Allow to stand for at least 30 minutes to blend the flavors.

The salsa will keep refrigerated for up to three days.

PICTURED ON PAGES XII-XIII, MIDDLE PHOTO

Sun-Dried Tomatoes

These are my signature wafer-thin dried tomatoes that I make in every one of my restaurants: fruity and slightly sweet, with just a hint of chewiness. If you keep them on hand, you'll be surprised how often you use them. **MAKES ABOUT 2 CUPS**

4 or 5 large firm plum tomatoes
About 2 cups mild olive oil

Line several large baking sheets with Silpats, rough side facing up. Slice the tomatoes paper-thin on a mandoline. Lay the slices out in rows on the Silpats. Do not worry about the seeds—they will dry along with the rest of the tomatoes.

Set the trays out in the sun to dry for a day, depending on the weather, or place the trays over or near a radiator. The edges will start to curl up, but when they are completely dry, they will be flat, crisp, and delicate.

Carefully lift the tomatoes one at a time off the Silpats and layer them in an airtight container or jar, covering them completely with olive oil. Store in the refrigerator for a week or more.

Salmuera

At its most basic, this is the saltwater solution—1 tablespoon salt to 1 cup water, boiled then cooled—gauchos use to baste their meat as it roasts or grills, whether it's a whole lamb on an iron cross, or a whole cow, or a smaller cut. Chimichurri is nothing more than a basic salmuera with oregano. The Mint-Chile Salmuera I serve with lamb and chicken and the Orange, Black Pepper, and Rosemary Salmuera I serve with pork are my own variations on this theme.

Mint-Chile Salmuera

Serve with lamb or chicken. **MAKES ABOUT 2 CUPS**

1 cup water
1 tablespoon coarse salt
1 teaspoon black peppercorns
3 garlic cloves, smashed and chopped
1 teaspoon grated lemon zest
2 tablespoons fresh lemon juice
1 small red or green chile pepper, seeded and chopped
1 cup fresh mint leaves, chopped
½ cup chopped fresh flat-leaf parsley
1 teaspoon crushed red pepper flakes
1 tablespoon red wine vinegar
½ cup extra virgin olive oil

Bring the water to a boil in a small saucepan. Add the salt and stir until it dissolves. Remove from the heat and let cool until tepid.

Meanwhile, wrap the peppercorns in a kitchen towel and pound with mallet until cracked. Place in a mortar, along with the garlic, lemon zest, juice, chopped chile, mint, parsley, and red pepper flakes and pound together to a rough paste. Whisk in the vinegar, half the salted water, and the olive oil. Taste for seasoning and stir in more salted water if desired. Let stand for 30 minutes to blend the flavors before serving.

Orange, Black Pepper, and Rosemary Salmuera

Serve with pork. **MAKES ABOUT 1½ CUPS**

1 cup water
1 tablespoon coarse salt, plus more to taste
1 navel orange
2 teaspoons black peppercorns
3 garlic cloves, roughly chopped
¼ cup fresh rosemary leaves, roughly chopped
1 tablespoon fresh lemon juice
¾ cup extra virgin olive oil

Bring the water to a boil in a small saucepan. Add the salt and stir until it dissolves. Remove from the heat.

Strip the zest from the orange, chop it, and set it aside in a mortar. Trim all the pith from the orange with a sharp paring knife and discard. Working over a small bowl to catch the juice, cut between the membranes to release the segments, letting them drop into the bowl. Then transfer the segments to a plate and reserve them separately.

Wrap the peppercorns in a kitchen towel and pound with a mallet until cracked. Add to the mortar, along with the garlic and rosemary, and pound together to a coarse paste.

Stir the rosemary mixture into the orange juice, then whisk in ¼ cup of the salted water, the lemon juice, and the olive oil. Transfer to a serving bowl, add the reserved orange segments, and season with salt to taste.

Rich Vegetable Stock

Vegetable stock can often be so shy that you hardly taste it. By increasing the proportion of vegetables to water, you create much more intensity of flavor.
MAKES ABOUT 4 QUARTS

2 medium onions, quartered
1 head garlic, cut horizontally in half
2 large leeks, split, thoroughly washed, and cut into 2-inch pieces
6 celery stalks with leaves, cut into chunks
3 medium carrots, peeled and quartered
2 bay leaves
12 black peppercorns
5 quarts water
Coarse salt and freshly ground black pepper

Put all the ingredients except the salt and pepper in a large stockpot and bring to a boil, then reduce the heat to low and cook, partially covered, for about 1 hour. Add salt, tasting carefully, and some pepper if you think it needs it.

Strain the stock through a sieve set over a large bowl, pressing down hard on the vegetables with a wooden spoon to extract all the flavor. Taste again and adjust the seasoning if necessary. Refrigerate for several days or freeze for up to 2 months.

Rich Brown
Pork Stock

When you buy a quarter pig for a *parrillada* or other large meal, you are going to end up with a lot of meat trimmings and bones. The bones are the foundation of one of my favorite stocks. Carefully browning them before making the stock and deglazing the roasting pan with red wine ensure deep color and flavor. The marrow from a piece of beef shin adds extra body.

MAKES ABOUT 5 QUARTS

4 pounds meaty pork bones and trimmings
One 1-pound beef shin, with marrow
2 medium onions, quartered
2 heads garlic, cut horizontally in half
2 large leeks, split, thoroughly washed, and cut into 2-inch pieces
6 celery stalks with leaves, cut into chunks
3 carrots, scrubbed and cut into chunks
4 bay leaves, preferably fresh
4 fresh rosemary sprigs
12 black peppercorns
Coarse salt and freshly ground black pepper
2 cups medium-bodied red wine, such as Uruguayan Tannat
About 6 quarts water

Heat an *horno* or the oven to 400°F.

Combine the bones, beef shin, vegetables, herbs, and peppercorns in one or two large roasting pans and season with salt and pepper. Roast for about 30 minutes, turning the bones and vegetables occasionally, until well browned.

Transfer the contents of the roasting pan to a large stockpot. Pour off any fat from the roasting pan, set over medium-low heat, and deglaze with the red wine, scraping up all the browned flavorful bits stuck to the bottom (or do this with both pans). Add this liquid to the stockpot, along with enough water to cover the solids by about 2 inches. Bring to a boil over medium heat, skimming off the foam as it rises to the top. When foam no longer rises, reduce the heat, add 1 tablespoon salt, and simmer gently for 3 hours, or until most of the meat has fallen off the bones and the liquid is very flavorful. Season with salt and pepper and turn off the heat.

When the bones are cool enough to handle, remove them from the pot. Pull off any remaining attached meat and return it to the stock. Set a large fine-mesh strainer over a large bowl and pour the stock through in batches, pressing down hard on the vegetables and meat with a wooden spoon to extract all the flavor. Taste for seasoning and refrigerate. When the stock is cool, skim off the fat. Refrigerate for several days or freeze for up to 2 months.

Crunchy Bread Crumbs

I prefer to make my own bread crumbs. Store-bought bread crumbs often contain flavorings I don't want, and even the plain ones are never as good as those made from scratch with good olive oil. The uneven size of these crumbs makes for a much more interesting crunch. **MAKES ABOUT 2½ CUPS**

8 ounces day-old bread, crust removed
2 tablespoons extra virgin olive oil
Salt and freshly ground black pepper

Preheat the oven to 375°F.

Crumble the bread into a bowl with your fingers, making small, uneven crumbs. Moisten with the olive oil and season with salt and pepper.

Turn the crumbs out onto a baking sheet and toast in the oven, tossing occasionally, for 8 to 10 minutes, until golden and crunchy. Let cool. Store in an airtight container at room temperature for up to 5 days.

Ember-Toasted Bread

By now you know that I love fire and I love toast. This toast brings the taste of fire directly into your mouth.
SERVES 4 TO 8

1 round country bread, such as a sourdough boule, sliced horizontally in half

Prepare a bed of coals. When the coals have turned completely white, place the bread crust side down on them. Watch carefully as it toasts—a matter of seconds—and once the crust side is toasted, turn it with tongs to toast the cut side.

When both sides are toasted, tear or cut each half into quarters. Top with ham or lardo while still warm.

SOME IMPORTANT TOOLS

The following items will make both cooking and grilling from this book much easier and more pleasant.

■ **Long heavy-duty heatproof gloves.**

■ **Long-handled fireplace tongs, shovel, poker, and hoe,** for moving and adjusting logs and live coals.

■ **Cast-iron and enameled cast-iron Dutch ovens (with lids),** for deep-frying as well as for stews and baked dishes.

■ **Earthenware baking dishes,** for casseroles, beans, and serving. I collect these on my travels. If properly cured, some earthenware can be used directly over low heat or adjacent to burning embers, as long as there are no abrupt temperature changes. Always ask the seller for instructions. A variety of *cazuelas* from Spain are available at www.tienda.com.

■ **A reversible large wooden carving board,** with a well on one side for meat juices.

■ **A digital instant-read thermometer** with a long wire probe will become your new best friend if you are not proficient at recognizing the look and feel of "doneness."

■ **Heavy-duty long-handled spring-action kitchen tongs.**

■ **Griddle scrapers (at least 3 inches wide):** These look like putty knives but are food-safe and great for flipping, turning, and removing food from the grill or *chapa*.

■ **A toolbox:** I use wrenches, wire cutters, and food-safe stainless steel wire for securing grill racks, trussing large cuts, or even suspending them from branches under which you have built a fire (see Leg of Lamb on Strings, page 109).

Some Ready-Made *Parrillas*
Once you have a fire, you need a grate. You can improvise your own or use a conventional kettle grill. Or, for ease of setup and the ability to add coals easily, here are some *parrillas* you can buy readymade.

■ **A 36-inch over-fire camp grill** provides a large surface area for use over a fire pit or a bed of coals on the ground.

■ **A Tuscan grill,** for setting over a bed of coals on the ground, can also be used in a fireplace.

■ For a big event, **a free-standing commercial charcoal grill,** which can be rented or bought, provides 10 square feet of grilling space.

For Grilling Indoors

■ **Cast-iron grill pan:** For those without access to an outdoor grill, a ridged cast-iron grill pan is an excellent alternative in a well-ventilated kitchen. The ridges should be deep enough to keep the food well above the fat that drains off into the grooves. The sides of the pan will keep the melted fat inside. A thick marbled steak will need a deeper pan with deeper ridges than, for example, sliced vegetables. The thickness of the ridges and the spacing between them determine the amount of char flavor and the look of the grill marks.

■ **A double-burner grill pan,** which can be set over two burners, offers more space for foods such as a butterflied leg of lamb or for cooking larger quantities.

For Grilling Fish or Vegetables on a *Parrilla*

■ **Grill baskets:** A hinged grill basket clamps around a fish, allowing it to be turned without sticking or breaking. An open metal grill basket, which sits on top of the grill grate, will keep smaller items from falling into the fire.

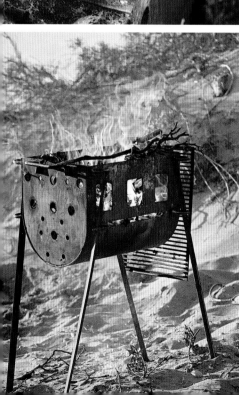

- **Jerky racks:** The wire racks from a smoker, such as a Camp Chef Smoke Vault, can be purchased separately from www.CampChef.com and used to help turn large fish that are too big for a regular grill basket. Set the fish between two oiled racks and secure them with wire.

Makeshift *Planchas* and *Chapas*

- **Cast-iron griddles:** A large cast-iron griddle can serve as a *chapa* both outdoors on a grill grate over a wood or charcoal fire or indoors over a conventional gas or electric burner. Indoors, use the largest size that will comfortably fit your burner; a 12-inch square griddle is a good size, and round ones (like old-fashioned pancake griddles) are also fine. Outdoors, a *chapa* can be set over just a portion of your grill space, allowing for two different cooking methods.

- **Cast-iron skillet:** A cast-iron skillet can be used indoors or outdoors as an extra *chapa*. It can also be used in an *horno* or a conventional oven as a roasting pan or as a substitute for a Brazilian iron box (see page 203). Get the largest size that will comfortably fit on your burner, as well as a smaller one for Spanish tortillas and for roasting potatoes. It is a very practical tool that allows you to sear or brown on the stovetop and then transfer to the oven for roasting.

My Portable Grill

My portable grill goes everywhere with me as I travel the world in search of inspiration. After a terrific fire cookout in Berkeley, California, I decided to make it a gift to my hostess, also a chef. When I got home to Argentina, it was back to the drawing board for another grill, pictured here. This time I elongated it to create more cooking surface. One oval functions as a *chapa* (aka *plancha*), the other as a *parrilla*, a simple grill. It suits me very well. Perhaps you know an iron maker who could make one for you. Or if I ever get down to the hard work of fabricating them myself, perhaps I'll be able to make them available.

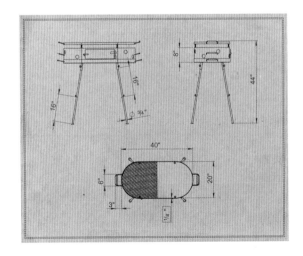

Peter, Donna, and me grilling in Peter's Brooklyn backyard.

OUR THANKS TO:

Mike Anthony and Danny Meyer of Gramercy Tavern

Noah and Rae Bernamoff of Mile End

Ann Bramson

Alejandro Bulgheroni of Wines of Garzón and Colinas de Garzón olive oil

CampChef.com

Vanina Chimeno

Jan Derevjanik

Ben Eisendrath of Grillworks

Josh Feigenbaum

Bruce Frankel of Spitjack

Mark Kelly of Lodge Manufacturing

Carlos Mallmann

Patrick Martins of Heritage Foods USA

Marta Matos

Richard and Barbara Moore

Buzzy O'Keefe of The River Café

Lisa Queen

Josefina Saubidet

Robert Service

Michael Silverstone

Pilar Soria

Andy Tarlow and Sean Rembold of Wythe Hotel and Reynard

Alice Waters

And the deepest gratitude to Peter Workman.

INDEX

aioli, basil, 75
Albondigas with Lentils, 94
almonds, Grilled Chilean Sea Bass with Toasted Almond Salsa, 181
amaretto:
 Burnt Peaches and Figs with Amaretto, Lemon Zest, and Mint, 243
 Grilled Bizcochuelo Strips with Amaretto and Burnt Shredded Quince, 244
anchovies:
 Eggplant a la Plancha with Cherry Tomatoes and Anchovies, 213
 Prawns, Sardines, and Anchovies a la Plancha with Zucchini, Swiss Chard, and Minted Yogurt, 196
apples, Butterflied Leg of Lamb with Rosemary and Thyme and Charred Apple Salsa, 115
Artagaveytia, Guzmán, 181
artichokes, Shaved Artichokes a la Plancha with Aged Comté Cheese, 39
Artichokes and Fingerling Potatoes a la Plancha, 229
arugula:
 Beet and Orange Salad with Arugula and Feta, 30
 Smashed Chicken Breast in a Potato Crust with Tomato and Arugula Salad, 148
asado, 9, 36
asparagus, Duck Breast with Balsamic Vinegar and Asparagus, 158
Asparagus Bundles Wrapped in Bacon with Fried Eggs, 72
avocadoes:
 Tomato and Avocado Salad, 33
 Tortilla of Prawns with Grilled Potatoes and Avocado, Chile Pepper, and Fennel Salsa, 69
 Tuna Churrasco and Avocado Sandwich, 78

Baby Turnips a la Plancha with Sun-Dried Tomatoes, 208

bacon:
 Asparagus Bundles Wrapped in Bacon with Fried Eggs, 72
 Potatoes with Smoked Pancetta, Leeks, Cream, and Cheese, 228
balsamic vinegar, Duck Breast with Balsamic Vinegar and Asparagus, 158
Bariloche, 8, 22
basil, Fig Salad with Burrata and Basil, 30
Basil Aioli, 75
bass:
 Grilled Chilean Sea Bass with Toasted Almond Salsa, 181
 Slashed and Stuffed Black Sea Bass with Potatoes, Leeks, and Mushrooms, 193
beans:
 Braised Beans with Red Wine and Tomato, 215
 Braised Black Beans, 216
 Creamy Polenta with Fresh Favas and Peas, 220
 Skate a la Plancha with Braised White Beans, Garlic, and Parsley, 174
 see also green beans
beef:
 Côte de Boeuf a la Parrilla with Maître d'Hôtel Butter, 98
 Grilled Short Ribs with Vinegar-Glazed Charred Endive, 101
 Red-Wine-Braised Spareribs with Red Cabbage and Carrot Slaw, 113
 Beet and Orange Salad with Arugula and Feta, 30
beets, Red and Golden Beet Salad with Radishes and Soft-Boiled Eggs, 26
berries:
 Broiled Sabayon with Berries, 251
 Pears with Malbec, Cream, and Berries, 251
 see also specific berries
Bizcochuelo, Grilled Bizcochuelo Strips with Amaretto and Burnt

Shredded Quince, 244
Black Bread with Nuts, 267
Blistered Peppers with Charred Onions and Lemon Zest, 45
blue cheese, Pear Salad with Mint, Blue Cheese, and Fresh Dates, 52
Braised Beans with Red Wine and Tomato, 215
Braised Black Beans, 216
Braised Carrots, 208
Braised Chorizo with Carrots, Fennel, and Creamy Polenta, 125
branzino, 193
Brazil, 235–36
bread:
 Black Bread with Nuts, 267
 Chapa Bread, 268
 Charred Mushrooms with Thyme and Garlic Toast, 22
 Cowboy Rib Eye a la Plancha with Crispy Brioche Salad and Grilled Dates, 97
 Crunchy Bread Crumbs, 290
 Ember-Toasted Bread, 290
 Ensalada de Sopa Paraguaya, 44
 Grilled Carrots with Aged Ricotta and Oregano on Toast, 25
 Huevos Escrachados with Pancetta, Zucchini Ribbons, and Green Peas, 64
 Pan de Molde, 266
 Tuna Tartare with Crunchy Bread Crumbs, 47
Broiled Sabayon with Berries, 251
Brooklyn, N.Y., 142
Bulgheroni, Alejandro, 282
Burnt Peaches and Figs with Amaretto, Lemon Zest, and Mint, 243
Burnt Shredded Quince, 245
burrata, 30
 Fig Salad with Burrata and Basil, 30
butter:
 Côte de Boeuf a la Parrilla with Maître d'Hôtel Butter, 98
 Mussels Steamed in Red Wine-

Butter Sauce with Shallots and
Parsley, 201
Butterflied Chicken a la Parrilla with
Chanterelles and Grilled Chicory,
149
Butterflied Leg of Lamb with
Rosemary and Thyme and
Charred Apple Salsa, 115

cabbage:
Red Cabbage and Carrot Slaw,
223
Red-Wine-Braised Spareribs with
Red Cabbage and Carrot Slaw,
133
Cabral, Pedro Alvares, 235
cachaça, 3
cake, pie:
Chocolate Torta del Lago with Nuts
and Dulce de Leche, 259
Grilled Bizcochuelo Strips with
Amaretto and Burnt Shredded
Quince, 244
Pionono with Dulce de Leche and
Strawberries, 249
Tarta of Cuartirolo Cheese and Red
Grapes, 264
Tarta de Picho, 264
calafate, 8
Calves' Liver a la Plancha with
Pimentón Oil, Onions, and
Crunchy Potatoes, 105
carciofi alia giudia, 39
carrots:
Braised Carrots, 208
Braised Chorizo with Carrots,
Fennel, and Creamy Polenta,
125
Grilled Carrots with Aged Ricotta
and Oregano on Toast, 25
Red Cabbage and Carrot Slaw,
223
Red-Wine-Braised Spareribs with
Red Cabbage and Carrot Slaw,
133
cauldron, 2, 152
celery, Shaved Hearts of Celery with
Portobello Mushrooms and

Meyer Lemon, 49, 51
chanterelles, Butterflied Chicken a la
Parrilla with Chanterelles and
Grilled Chicory, 149
Chapa Bread, 268
chapa (plancha), 2, 8, 13, 17, 18, 19,
36, 42, 274, 294
Artichokes and Fingerling Potatoes
a la Plancha, 229
Baby Turnips a la Plancha with
Sun-Dried Tomatoes, 208
Calves' Liver a la Plancha with
Pimentón Oil, Onions, and
Crunchy Potatoes, 105
Chicken Livers a la Plancha in
Charred Endive, 42
Cowboy Rib Eye a la Plancha with
Crispy Brioche Salad and Grilled
Dates, 97
Eggplant a la Plancha with Cherry
Tomatoes and Anchovies, 213
Hake Steaks a la Plancha with
Fried Potatoes and Garlic, 192
Prawns, Sardines, and Anchovies
a la Plancha with Zucchini, Swiss
Chard, and Minted Yogurt, 196
Shaved Artichokes a la Plancha
with Aged Comté Cheese, 39
Skate a la Plancha with Braised
White Beans, Garlic, and Parsley,
174
Sliced Kidney Strips a la Plancha
with Salsa Provenzal, 104
use of, 14
Veal Rib Chops and French
Green Beans a la Plancha with
Romaine-Watercress Salad, 93
Chapel, Alain, 57, 61
charcoal, 8, 19
adding more, 17–18
charcoal, hardwood lump, 17
chard:
Churrasco of Tuna with Coal-Burnt
Pimentón Oil, Heirloom Tomato
and Chard Salad, and Garlicky
Potato Puree, 170–71
Coal-Roasted Zucchini and Swiss
Chard, 223

Octopus in an Iron Box with Chard,
Green Beans, Tomatoes, and
Eggs, 203
Prawns, Sardines, and Anchovies
a la Plancha with Zucchini, Swiss
Chard, and Minted Yogurt, 196
Charred Herb Salsa, 122
Charred Mushrooms with Thyme and
Garlic Toast, 22
cheese:
Beet and Orange Salad with
Arugula and Feta, 30
Eggplants Stuffed with Tomatoes
and Cuartirolo Cheese, 214
Endive Salad with Mustard, Aged
Goat Cheese, and Toasted
Walnuts, 52
Fig Salad with Burrata and Basil, 30
Gratin of Potatoes with Emmental
Wrapped in Bayonne Ham, 226
Griddled Cheeses with Parsley,
Red Onion, and Cherry
Tomatoes, 36
Grilled Carrots with Aged Ricotta
and Oregano on Toast, 25
Pear Salad with Mint, Blue Cheese,
and Fresh Dates, 52
Potatoes with Smoked Pancetta,
Leeks, Cream, and Cheese, 228
Shaved Artichokes a la Plancha
with Aged Comté Cheese, 39
Tarta of Cuartirolo Cheese and Red
Grapes, 264
Chez Panisse, 26, 176
chicken:
Butterflied Chicken a la Parrilla with
Chanterelles and Grilled Chicory,
149
Crisp Chicken Skin, Lettuce, and
Heirloom Tomato Sandwich, 75
Griddled Chicken with Charred
Herb and Tomato Salad, 157
Smashed Chicken Breast in a
Potato Crust with Tomato and
Arugula Salad, 148
Chicken Livers a la Plancha in
Charred Endive, 42
Chicken on Strings, 109

chicory, Butterflied Chicken a la
Parrilla with Chanterelles and
Grilled Chicory, 149
chile pepper:
Leg of Lamb on Strings with Mint-
Chile Salmuera, 109
Mint-Chile Salmuera, 287
Tortilla of Prawns with Grilled
Potatoes and Avocado, Chile
Pepper, and Fennel Salsa, 69
Chilled Flavored Olive Oil, 281
Chocolate Torta del Lago with Nuts
and Dulce de Leche, 259
chorizo, Braised Chorizo with Carrots,
Fennel, and Creamy Polenta, 125
Chupin de Pescado, 200
churrasco, 78
Churrasco of Tuna with Coal-Burnt
Pimentón Oil, Heirloom Tomato
and Chard Salad, and Garlicky
Potato Puree, 170–71
coal, *see* charcoal
Coal-Burnt Pimentón Oil, 171
Coal-Roasted Zucchini and Swiss
Chard, 223
Comté cheese, Shaved Artichokes
a la Plancha with Aged Comté
Cheese, 39
cooking stones, ix
Côte de Boeuf a la Parrilla with Maître
d'Hôtel Butter, 98
Cowboy Rib Eye a la Plancha with
Crispy Brioche Salad and Grilled
Dates, 97
cream:
Pears with Malbec, Cream, and
Berries, 251
Potatoes with Smoked Pancetta,
Leeks, Cream, and Cheese, 228
Creamy Polenta with Fresh Favas and
Peas, 220
Crisp Chicken Skin, Lettuce, and
Heirloom Tomato Sandwich, 75
Crunchy Bread Crumbs, 290
Tuna Tartare with Crunchy Bread
Crumbs, 47
Crunchy Potato Skins with Parsley, 45
Crusty Rice, 219
Cuartirolo cheese:
Eggplants Stuffed with Tomatoes
and Cuartirolo Cheese, 214
Tarta of Cuartirolo Cheese and Red
Grapes, 263
curanto, 8, 277

dates:
Cowboy Rib Eye a la Plancha with

Crispy Brioche Salad and Grilled
Dates, 97
Pear Salad with Mint, Blue Cheese,
and Fresh Dates, 52
Duck Breast with Balsamic Vinegar
and Asparagus, 158
dulce de leche:
Chocolate Torta del Lago with Nuts
and Dulce de Leche, 259
Pionono with Dulce de Leche and
Strawberries, 249
Dulce de Leche Ice Cream, 258

Eggplant a la Plancha with Cherry
Tomatoes and Anchovies, 213
Eggplants Stuffed with Tomatoes and
Cuartirolo Cheese, 214
eggs:
Asparagus Bundles Wrapped in
Bacon with Fried Eggs, 72
Huevos Escrachados with
Pancetta, Zucchini Ribbons, and
Green Peas, 64
Octopus in an Iron Box with Chard,
Green Beans, Tomatoes, and
Eggs, 203
Red and Golden Beet Salad with
Radishes and Soft-Boiled Eggs,
26
Ember-Toasted Bread, 290
Emmental, Gratin of Potatoes with
Emmental Wrapped in Bayonne
Ham, 226
endives:
Chicken Livers a la Plancha in
Charred Endive, 42
Grilled Short Ribs with Vinegar-
Glazed Charred Endive, 101
Endive Salad with Mustard, Aged
Goat Cheese, and Toasted
Walnuts, 52
Ensalada de Sopa Paraguaya, 44

favas, Creamy Polenta with Fresh
Favas and Peas, 220
fennel:
Braised Chorizo with Carrots,
Fennel, and Creamy Polenta,
125
Grilled Whole Fish Stuffed with
Fennel, 176–77
Tortilla of Prawns with Grilled
Potatoes and Avocado, Chile
Pepper, and Fennel Salsa, 69
feta, Beet and Orange Salad with
Arugula and Feta, 30
figs, Burnt Peaches and Figs with

Amaretto, Lemon Zest, and Mint,
243
Fig Salad with Burrata and Basil, 30
fire cooking:
in brick or clay oven (*horno*), 15
cinder blocks for, 14
coals for, 8, 17–18
on embers and ashes (*rescoldo*),
15
feeding the fire, 17
of fish, 183
heat as important to, 14, 15
important tools for, 292–94
Indians and, ix, 2–3, 8, 13, 17, 102,
141–42, 236, 274
meat and, 18, 116, 119
parrillada, 116–21
safety for, 18
in the snow, 152
vegetables and, 18, 116, 119, 152
wooden stakes for, 8
see also specific cooking materials
fish, shellfish:
Chupin de Pescado, 200
Churrasco of Tuna with Coal-Burnt
Pimentón Oil, Heirloom Tomato
and Chard Salad, and Garlicky
Potato Puree, 170
Eggplant a la Plancha with Cherry
Tomatoes and Anchovies, 213
Grilled Chilean Sea Bass with
Toasted Almond Salsa, 181
Grilled Dover Sole with Parsleyed
Boiled Potatoes, 188
Grilled Giant Flatfish Stuffed with
Peppers, Onions, and Herbs,
185–86
Grilled Whole Fish Stuffed with
Fennel, 176–77
Hake Steaks a la Plancha with
Fried Potatoes and Garlic, 192
Mussels Steamed in Red Wine-
Butter Sauce with Shallots and
Parsley, 201
Octopus in an Iron Box with Chard,
Green Beans, Tomatoes, and
Eggs, 203
Prawns, Sardines, and Anchovies
a la Plancha with Zucchini, Swiss
Chard, and Minted Yogurt, 196
Skate a la Plancha with Braised
White Beans, Garlic, and Parsley,
174
Slashed and Stuffed Black Sea
Bass with Potatoes, Leeks, and
Mushrooms, 193
Split Lobster a la Parrilla with

Scallops, 204
sticks to grill, 183
Surf and Swine, 197
Tortilla of Prawns with Grilled
    Potatoes and Avocado, Chile
    Pepper, and Fennel Salsa, 69
Tuna Churrasco and Avocado
    Sandwich, 78
Tuna Tartare with Crunchy Bread
    Crumbs, 47
flatfish:
    Grilled Dover Sole with Parsleyed
        Boiled Potatoes, 188
    Grilled Giant Flatfish Stuffed with
        Peppers, Onions, and Herbs,
        185–86

garlic:
    Charred Mushrooms with Thyme
        and Garlic Toast, 22
    Churrasco of Tuna with Coal-Burnt
        Pimentón Oil, Heirloom Tomato
        and Chard Salad, and Garlicky
        Potato Puree, 170–71
    Hake Steaks a la Plancha with
        Fried Potatoes and Garlic, 192
    Skate a la Plancha with Braised
        White Beans, Garlic, and Parsley,
        174
    Weeping Lamb, 108
Garzón, 26, 103, 163–64
gauchos, 15, 76, 268
Gelb, Donna, 282
goat cheese, Endive Salad with
    Mustard, Aged Goat Cheese,
    and Toasted Walnuts, 52
gooseberry, Sabayon Ice Cream
    with Roasted Pineapple and
    Gooseberry Jelly, 254
Grand Véfour, 57
grapes:
    Pork Loin Chops with Thyme Oil
        and Roasted Grapes on the
        Vine, 134
    Roasted Grapes on the Vine, 282
    Tarta of Cuartirolo Cheese and Red
        Grapes, 263
Gratin of Potatoes with Emmental
    Wrapped in Bayonne Ham, 226
Gray, Rose, 229
green beans:
    Octopus in an Iron Box with Chard,
        Green Beans, Tomatoes, and
        Eggs, 203
    Veal Rib Chops and French
        Green Beans a la Plancha with
        Romaine-Watercress Salad, 93

Griddled Cheeses with Parsley, Red
    Onion, and Cherry Tomatoes, 36
Griddled Chicken with Charred Herb
    and Tomato Salad, 157
Griddled Red Bartlett Pears Wrapped
    in Iberico Ham, 33
Grilled Bizcochuelo Strips with
    Amaretto and Burnt Shredded
    Quince, 244
Grilled Carrots with Aged Ricotta and
    Oregano on Toast, 25
Grilled Chilean Sea Bass with Toasted
    Almond Salsa, 181
Grilled Dover Sole with Parsleyed
    Boiled Potatoes, 188
Grilled Giant Flatfish Stuffed with
    Peppers, Onions, and Herbs,
    185–86
Grilled and Roasted Leg of Pork
    Wrapped in Rosemary with
    Orange, Black Pepper, and
    Rosemary Salmuera, 129
Grilled Short Ribs with Vinegar-Glazed
    Charred Endive, 101
Grilled Skirt Steak Sandwich with
    Watercress, Onion, Tomato, and
    Mustard, 76
Grilled Whole Fish Stuffed with
    Fennel, 176–77

Hake Steaks a la Plancha with Fried
    Potatoes and Garlic, 192
ham:
    Gratin of Potatoes with Emmental
        Wrapped in Bayonne Ham, 226
    Griddled Red Bartlett Pears
        Wrapped in Iberico Ham, 33
hardwood lump charcoal, 17
hearts of celery, Shaved Hearts
    of Celery with Portobello
    Mushrooms and Meyer Lemon,
    49, 51
heat levels, 14, 15, 17
Hemingway, Ernest, 57
herbs:
    Charred Herb Salsa, 122
    Griddled Chicken with Charred
        Herb and Tomato Salad, 157
    Grilled Giant Flatfish Stuffed with
        Peppers, Onions, and Herbs,
        185–86
    see also specific herbs
horno (brick or clay oven), 15, 274
Huevos Escrachados with Pancetta,
    Zucchini Ribbons, and Green
    Peas, 64

ice cream:
    Dulce de Leche Ice Cream, 258
    Sabayon Ice Cream with Roasted
        Pineapple and Gooseberry Jelly,
        254
infiernillo, 2, 8
iron, 17
    cast-, 14
    cleaning of, 17

jelly:
    Open-Faced Pomegranate Jelly
        and Lardo Sandwich, 81
    Sabayon Ice Cream with Roasted
        Pineapple and Gooseberry Jelly,
        254
José Ignacio, 163, 181

Kaminsky, Peter, 1, 9, 109
kidney, Sliced Kidney Strips a la
        Plancha with Salsa Provenzal,
        104

lamb:
    Butterflied Leg of Lamb with
        Rosemary and Thyme and
        Charred Apple Salsa, 115
    Leg of Lamb with Merguez, Coal-
        Roasted Delicata Squash, and
        Orange, Black Pepper, and
        Rosemary Salmuera, 112
    Leg of Lamb on Strings with Mint-
        Chile Salmuera, 109
    Weeping Lamb, 108
lardo, Open-Faced Pomegranate Jelly
    and Lardo Sandwich, 81
Ledoyen, 57
leeks:
    Potatoes with Smoked Pancetta,
        Leeks, Cream, and Cheese, 228
    Slashed and Stuffed Black Sea
        Bass with Potatoes, Leeks, and
        Mushrooms, 193
Leg of Lamb with Merguez, Coal-
    Roasted Delicata Squash, and
    Orange, Black Pepper, and
    Rosemary Salmuera, 112
Leg of Lamb on Strings with Mint-
    Chile Salmuera, 109
lemon:
    Blistered Peppers with Charred
        Onions and Lemon Zest, 45
    Burnt Peaches and Figs with
        Amaretto, Lemon Zest, and Mint,
        243
    Shaved Hearts of Celery with
        Portobello Mushrooms and

Meyer Lemon, 49, 51
lentils, Albondigas with Lentils, 94
lettuce:
    Crisp Chicken Skin, Lettuce, and
        Heirloom Tomato Sandwich, 75
    Veal Rib Chops and French
        Green Beans a la Plancha with
        Romaine-Watercress Salad, 93
livers:
    Calves' Liver a la Plancha with
        Pimentón Oil, Onions, and
        Crunchy Potatoes, 105
    Chicken Livers a la Plancha in
        Charred Endive, 42
lobster, Split Lobster a la Parrilla with
    Scallops, 204
López, Carlos Antonio, 44

Maître d'Hôtel Butter, Côte de Boeuf
    a la Parrilla with Maître d'Hôtel
    Butter, 98
Malbec, Pears with Malbec, Cream,
    and Berries, 251
Mallmann, Carlos, 8, 251, 273
Mallmann, Eloisa, 236
Mallmann, Francis, 1, 2–3
    aesthetic of, 1, 3
    background of, 7–8
    cooking method of, 3
    custom grill of, 13, 17
    travels of, 8–9, 141–42, 163–64,
        235–36
    TV show of, ix, 13, 52, 75
Mallmann, Vanina, 2, 235
Marcial (Mallmann's friend), 273
Mary's Fish Camp, 45
meat, fire cooking and, 18, 116, 119
meatballs, Albondigas with Lentils, 94
Mecha (Mallmann's aunt), 264
merguez, Leg of Lamb with Merguez,
    Coal-Roasted Delicata Squash,
    and Orange, Black Pepper, and
    Rosemary Salmuera, 112
milanesa, 148
mint:
    Burnt Peaches and Figs with
        Amaretto, Lemon Zest, and Mint,
        243
    Pear Salad with Mint, Blue Cheese,
        and Fresh Dates, 52
    Prawns, Sardines, and Anchovies
        a la Plancha with Zucchini, Swiss
        Chard, and Minted Yogurt, 196
Mint-Chile Salmuera, 287
    Leg of Lamb on Strings with Mint-
        Chile Salmuera, 109
mushrooms:

Charred Mushrooms with Thyme
    and Garlic Toast, 22
Shaved Hearts of Celery with
    Portobello Mushrooms and
    Meyer Lemon, 49, 51
Slashed and Stuffed Black Sea
    Bass with Potatoes, Leeks, and
    Mushrooms, 193
umami flavor of, 22, 49
Mussels Steamed in Red Wine-Butter
    Sauce with Shallots and Parsley,
    201
mustard:
    Endive Salad with Mustard, Aged
        Goat Cheese, and Toasted
        Walnuts, 52
    Grilled Skirt Steak Sandwich with
        Watercress, Onion, Tomato, and
        Mustard, 76

New York, N.Y., 141–42
nuts:
    Black Bread with Nuts, 267
    Chocolate Torta del Lago with Nuts
        and Dulce de Leche, 259
    Endive Salad with Mustard, Aged
        Goat Cheese, and Toasted
        Walnuts, 52
    Grilled Chilean Sea Bass with
        Toasted Almond Salsa, 181
    Pork Chops with Toasted Nuts, 128
    Toasted Nuts, 283
    Toasted Nut Salsa, 283

Octopus in an Iron Box with Chard,
    Green Beans, Tomatoes, and
    Eggs, 203
oil:
    Calves' Liver a la Plancha with
        Pimentón Oil, Onions, and
        Crunchy Potatoes, 105
    Chilled Flavored Olive Oil, 281
    Churrasco of Tuna with Coal-Burnt
        Pimentón Oil, Heirloom Tomato
        and Chard Salad, and Garlicky
        Potato Puree, 170
    Pimentón Oil, 171, 281
    Pork Loin Chops with Thyme Oil
        and Roasted Grapes on the
        Vine, 134
olives, olive oil:
    Chilled Flavored Olive Oil, 281
    Potato Salad with Black Olives, 48
olla de barro, 226
onions:
    Beet and Orange Salad with
        Arugula and Feta, 30

Blistered Peppers with Charred
    Onions and Lemon Zest, 45
Calves' Liver a la Plancha with
    Pimentón Oil, Onions, and
    Crunchy Potatoes, 105
Griddled Cheeses with Parsley,
    Red Onion, and Cherry
    Tomatoes, 36
Grilled Giant Flatfish Stuffed with
    Peppers, Onions, and Herbs,
    185–86
Grilled Skirt Steak Sandwich with
    Watercress, Onion, Tomato, and
    Mustard, 76
Open-Faced Pomegranate Jelly and
    Lardo Sandwich, 81
Orange, Black Pepper, and Rosemary
    Salmuera, 287
Grilled and Roasted Leg of Pork
    Wrapped in Rosemary with
    Orange, Black Pepper, and
    Rosemary Salmuera, 129
Leg of Lamb with Merguez, Coal-
    Roasted Delicata Squash, and
    Orange, Black Pepper, and
    Rosemary Salmuera, 112
oranges, Beet and Orange Salad with
    Arugula and Feta, 30
oregano, Grilled Carrots with Aged
    Ricotta and Oregano on Toast, 25

pancetta:
    Huevos Escrachados with
        Pancetta, Zucchini Ribbons, and
        Green Pease, 64
    Potatoes with Smoked Pancetta,
        Leeks, Cream, and Cheese, 228
Pan de Molde, 266
Paris, 57–61, 174
parrillada, 116–21
    preparation timeframe for, 120–21
Parrillada of Pork and Vegetables,
    116–21
parrilla (grill), 2, 13, 19, 274, 292
    Butterflied Chicken a la Parrilla with
        Chanterelles and Grilled Chicory,
        149
    Côte de Boeuf a la Parrilla with
        Maître d'Hôtel Butter, 98
    Split Lobster a la Parrilla with
        Scallops, 204
    use of, 14
parsley:
    Crunchy Potato Skins with Parsley,
        45
    Griddled Cheeses with Parsley,
        Red Onion, and Cherry

Tomatoes, 36
Grilled Dover Sole with Parsleyed
    Boiled Potatoes, 188
Mussels Steamed in Red Wine-
    Butter Sauce with Shallots and
    Parsley, 201
Skate a la Plancha with Braised
    White Beans, Garlic, and Parsley,
    174
Patagonia, 1, 7–8, 18, 22, 85–86, 174,
    273–77
The Island in, 273–74
peaches, Burnt Peaches and Figs
    with Amaretto, Lemon Zest, and
    Mint, 243
pears:
    Griddled Red Bartlett Pears
        Wrapped in Iberico Ham, 33
    Pressed Pears and Plums in Red
        Wine with Rosemary, 258
Pear Salad with Mint, Blue Cheese,
    and Fresh Dates, 52
Pears with Malbec, Cream, and
    Berries, 251
peas:
    Creamy Polenta with Fresh Favas
        and Peas, 220
    Huevos Escrachados with
        Pancetta, Zucchini Ribbons, and
        Green Peas, 64
pepper:
    Grilled and Roasted Leg of Pork
        Wrapped in Rosemary with
        Orange, Black Pepper, and
        Rosemary Salmuera, 129
    Leg of Lamb with Merguez, Coal-
        Roasted Delicata Squash, and
        Orange, Black Pepper, and
        Rosemary Salmuera, 112
    Orange, Black Pepper, and
        Rosemary Salmuera, 287
    Tortilla of Prawns with Grilled
        Potatoes and Avocado, Chile
        Pepper, and Fennel Salsa, 69
peppers:
    Blistered Peppers with Charred
        Onions and Lemon Zest, 45
    Grilled Giant Flatfish Stuffed with
        Peppers, Onions, and Herbs,
        185–86
picadas, 36
Picho (Mallmann's mother), 264
Pimentón Oil, 171, 281
    Calves' Liver a la Plancha with
        Pimentón Oil, Onions, and
        Crunchy Potatoes, 105
    Churrasco of Tuna with Coal-Burnt

Pimentón Oil, Heirloom Tomato
    and Chard Salad, and Garlicky
    Potato Puree, 170
pimientos de Padrón, 45
pineapples, Sabayon Ice Cream
    with Roasted Pineapple and
    Gooseberry Jelly, 254
Pionono with Dulce de Leche and
    Strawberries, 249
plancha, see chapa (plancha)
plums, Pressed Pears and Plums in
    Red Wine with Rosemary, 258
polenta:
    Braised Chorizo with Carrots,
        Fennel, and Creamy Polenta,
        125
    Creamy Polenta with Fresh Favas
        and Peas, 220
pomegranate, Open-Faced
    Pomegranate Jelly and Lardo
    Sandwich, 81
pork, 116
    Grilled and Roasted Leg of Pork
        Wrapped in Rosemary with
        Orange, Black Pepper, and
        Rosemary Salmuera, 129
    Parrillada of Pork and Vegetables,
        116–21
    Red-Wine-Braised Spareribs with
        Red Cabbage and Carrot Slaw,
        113
    Rich Brown Pork Stock, 289
    Surf and Swine, 197
Pork Chops with Toasted Nuts, 128
Pork Loin Chops with Thyme Oil and
    Roasted Grapes on the Vine, 134
portobello mushrooms, Shaved
    Hearts of Celery with Portobello
    Mushrooms and Meyer Lemon,
    49, 51
potatoes:
    Artichokes and Fingerling Potatoes
        a la Plancha, 229
    Calves' Liver a la Plancha with
        Pimentón Oil, Onions, and
        Crunchy Potatoes, 105
    Churrasco of Tuna with Coal-Burnt
        Pimentón Oil, Heirloom Tomato
        and Chard Salad, and Garlicky
        Potato Puree, 170–71
    Crunchy Potato Skins with Parsley,
        45
    Gratin of Potatoes with Emmental
        Wrapped in Bayonne Ham, 226
    Grilled Dover Sole with Parsleyed
        Boiled Potatoes, 188
    Hake Steaks a la Plancha with

Fried Potatoes and Garlic, 192
Slashed and Stuffed Black Sea
    Bass with Potatoes, Leeks, and
    Mushrooms, 193
Smashed Chicken Breast in a
    Potato Crust with Tomato and
    Arugula Salad, 148
Smashed Potatoes, 228
Tortilla of Cast-Iron Fried Potatoes,
    Spinach, and Sun-Dried
    Tomatoes, 65
Tortilla of Prawns with Grilled
    Potatoes and Avocado, Chile
    Pepper, and Fennel Salsa, 69
Potatoes with Smoked Pancetta,
    Leeks, Cream, and Cheese, 228
Potato Salad with Black Olives, 48
Prawns, Sardines, and Anchovies a
    la Plancha with Zucchini, Swiss
    Chard, and Minted Yogurt, 196
prawns, Tortilla of Prawns with Grilled
    Potatoes and Avocado, Chile
    Pepper, and Fennel Salsa, 69
Pressed Pears and Plums in Red
    Wine with Rosemary, 258

quince:
    Burnt Shredded Quince, 245
    Grilled Bizcochuelo Strips with
        Amaretto and Burnt Shredded
        Quince, 244

radishes, Red and Golden Beet Salad
    with Radishes and Soft-Boiled
    Eggs, 26
Red Cabbage and Carrot Slaw, 223
Red and Golden Beet Salad with
    Radishes and Soft-Boiled Eggs,
    26
Red-Wine-Braised Spareribs with Red
    Cabbage and Carrot Slaw, 133
rescoldo (embers and ashes), 15
rice, Crusty Rice, 219
Rich Brown Pork Stock, 289
Rich Vegetable Stock, 288
ricotta, Grilled Carrots with Aged
    Ricotta and Oregano on Toast,
    25
River Café, 229, 283
Roasted Grapes on the Vine, 282
    Pork Loin Chops with Thyme Oil
        and Roasted Grapes on the
        Vine, 134
Roberta's, 101
Romaine lettuce, Veal Rib Chops
    and French Green Beans a
    la Plancha with Romaine-

Watercress Salad, 93
rosemary:
  Butterflied Leg of Lamb with
    Rosemary and Thyme and
    Charred Apple Salsa, 115
  Grilled and Roasted Leg of Pork
    Wrapped in Rosemary with
    Orange, Black Pepper, and
    Rosemary Salmuera, 129
  Leg of Lamb with Merguez, Coal-
    Roasted Delicata Squash, and
    Orange, Black Pepper, and
    Rosemary Salmuera, 112
  Orange, Black Pepper, and
    Rosemary Salmuera, 287
  Pressed Pears and Plums in Red
    Wine with Rosemary, 258

Sabayon, Broiled Sabayon with
  Berries, 251
Sabayon Ice Cream with Roasted Pine-
  apple and Gooseberry Jelly, 254
salad:
  Beet and Orange Salad with
    Arugula and Feta, 30
  Churrasco of Tuna with Coal-Burnt
    Pimentón Oil, Heirloom Tomato
    and Chard Salad, and Garlicky
    Potato Puree, 170–71
  Cowboy Rib Eye a la Plancha with
    Crispy Brioche Salad and Grilled
    Dates, 97
  Endive Salad with Mustard, Aged
    Goat Cheese, and Toasted
    Walnuts, 52
  Ensalada de Sopa Paraguaya, 44
  Fig Salad with Burrata and Basil,
    30
  Griddled Chicken with Charred
    Herb and Tomato Salad, 157
  Pear Salad with Mint, Blue Cheese,
    and Fresh Dates, 52
  Potato Salad with Black Olives, 48
  Red and Golden Beet Salad with
    Radishes and Soft-Boiled Eggs,
    26
  Smashed Chicken Breast in a
    Potato Crust with Tomato and
    Arugula Salad, 148
  Tomato and Avocado Salad, 33
  Veal Rib Chops and French
    Green Beans a la Plancha with
    Romaine-Watercress Salad, 93
Salmuera, 287
  Grilled and Roasted Leg of Pork
    Wrapped in Rosemary with
    Orange, Black Pepper, and

Rosemary Salmuera, 129
Leg of Lamb with Merguez, Coal-
  Roasted Delicata Squash, and
  Orange, Black Pepper, and
  Rosemary Salmuera, 112
Leg of Lamb on Strings with Mint-
  Chile Salmuera, 109
Mint-Chile Salmuera, 287
Orange, Black Pepper, and
  Rosemary Salmuera, 287
salsa:
  Butterflied Leg of Lamb with
    Rosemary and Thyme and
    Charred Apple Salsa, 115
  Charred Herb Salsa, 122
  Grilled Chilean Sea Bass with
    Toasted Almond Salsa, 181
  Sliced Kidney Strips a la Plancha
    with Salsa Provenzal, 104
  Toasted Nut Salsa, 283
  Tortilla of Prawns with Grilled
    Potatoes and Avocado, Chile
    Pepper, and Fennel Salsa, 69
Salsa Criolla, 285
Salsa Llajua, 284
Salsa Provenzal, 284
San Domenico, 30
sandwiches:
  Crisp Chicken Skin, Lettuce, and
    Heirloom Tomato Sandwich, 75
  Grilled Skirt Steak Sandwich with
    Watercress, Onion, Tomato, and
    Mustard, 76
  Open-Faced Pomegranate Jelly
    and Lardo Sandwich, 81
  Tuna Churrasco and Avocado
    Sandwich, 78
sardines, Prawns, Sardines, and
    Anchovies a la Plancha with
    Zucchini, Swiss Chard, and
    Minted Yogurt, 196
sausages:
  Braised Chorizo with Carrots,
    Fennel, and Creamy Polenta,
    125
  Leg of Lamb with Merguez, Coal-
    Roasted Delicata Squash, and
    Orange, Black Pepper, and
    Rosemary Salmuera, 112
scallops, Split Lobster a la Parrilla with
    Scallops, 204
Scarpetti, Tomas, 47
Scones from The Teapot, 268
Senderens, Alain, 57
Serra, Richard, 2
shallots, Mussels Steamed in Red
    Wine-Butter Sauce with Shallots

and Parsley, 201
Shaved Artichokes a la Plancha with
    Aged Comté Cheese, 39
Shaved Hearts of Celery with
    Portobello Mushrooms and
    Meyer Lemon, 49, 51
short ribs, Grilled Short Ribs with
    Vinegar-Glazed Charred Endive,
    101
shrimp:
  Prawns, Sardines, and Anchovies
    a la Plancha with Zucchini, Swiss
    Chard, and Minted Yogurt, 196
  Tortilla of Prawns with Grilled
    Potatoes and Avocado, Chile
    Pepper, and Fennel Salsa, 69
Simple Syrup, 244
Skate a la Plancha with Braised White
    Beans, Garlic, and Parsley, 174
Slashed and Stuffed Black Sea
    Bass with Potatoes, Leeks, and
    Mushrooms, 193
slaw:
  Red Cabbage and Carrot Slaw,
    223
  Red-Wine-Braised Spareribs with
    Red Cabbage and Carrot Slaw,
    133
Sliced Kidney Strips a la Plancha with
    Salsa Provenzal, 104
Smashed Chicken Breast in a Potato
    Crust with Tomato and Arugula
    Salad, 148
Smashed Potatoes, 228
snow, 152
sole, Grilled Dover Sole with
    Parsleyed Boiled Potatoes, 188
Sopa Paraguaya, 44, 266
Soria, Pilar, 266
spareribs, Red-Wine-Braised
    Spareribs with Red Cabbage
    and Carrot Slaw, 133
spinach, Tortilla of Cast-Iron Fried
    Potatoes, Spinach, and Sun-
    Dried Tomatoes, 65
Split Lobster a la Parrilla with
    Scallops, 204
squash, Leg of Lamb with Merguez,
    Coal-Roasted Delicata Squash,
    and Orange, Black Pepper, and
    Rosemary Salmuera, 112
steak:
  Côte de Boeuf a la Parrilla with
    Maître d'Hôtel Butter, 98
  Cowboy Rib Eye a la Plancha with
    Crispy Brioche Salad and Grilled
    Dates, 97

Grilled Skirt Steak Sandwich with
Watercress, Onion, Tomato, and
Mustard, 76
stew, Chupin de Pescado, 200
stock:
Rich Brown Pork Stock, 289
Rich Vegetable Stock, 288
strawberries, Pionono with Dulce de
Leche and Strawberries, 249
Sun-Dried Tomatoes, 285
Baby Turnips a la Plancha with
Sun-Dried Tomatoes, 208
Tortilla of Cast-Iron Fried Potatoes,
Spinach, and Sun-Dried
Tomatoes, 65
Surf and Swine, 197
Swiss chard:
Coal-Roasted Zucchini and Swiss
Chard, 223
Prawns, Sardines, and Anchovies
a la Plancha with Zucchini, Swiss
Chard, and Minted Yogurt, 196
syrup, Simple Syrup, 244

Taillevent, 57
Tanis, David, 26
Tarta of Cuartirolo Cheese and Red
Grapes, 263
Tarta de Picho, 263
Tata (Mallman's grandmother), 251
Teapot, The, 264
textiles, 3, 246
Thuilier, Raymond, 228
thyme:
Butterflied Leg of Lamb with
Rosemary and Thyme and
Charred Apple Salsa, 115
Charred Mushrooms with Thyme
and Garlic Toast, 22
Pork Loin Chops with Thyme Oil
and Roasted Grapes on the
Vine, 134
Toasted Almond Salsa, 181
Toasted Nuts, 283
Endive Salad with Mustard, Aged
Goat Cheese, and Toasted
Walnuts, 52
Grilled Chilean Sea Bass with
Toasted Almond Salsa, 181
Pork Chops with Toasted Nuts, 128
Toasted Nut Salsa, 283
Tocellier, Francis, 52
Tomato and Avocado Salad, 33
tomatoes:
Baby Turnips a la Plancha with
Sun-Dried Tomatoes, 208
Braised Beans with Red Wine and

Tomato, 215
Churrasco of Tuna with Coal-Burnt
Pimentón Oil, Heirloom Tomato
and Chard Salad, and Garlicky
Potato Puree, 170–71
Crisp Chicken Skin, Lettuce, and
Heirloom Tomato Sandwich, 75
Eggplant a la Plancha with Cherry
Tomatoes and Anchovies, 213
Eggplants Stuffed with Tomatoes
and Cuartirolo Cheese, 214
Griddled Cheeses with Parsley,
Red Onion, and Cherry
Tomatoes, 36
Griddled Chicken with Charred
Herb and Tomato Salad, 157
Grilled Skirt Steak Sandwich with
Watercress, Onion, Tomato, and
Mustard, 76
Octopus in an Iron Box with Chard,
Green Beans, Tomatoes, and
Eggs, 203
Smashed Chicken Breast in a
Potato Crust with Tomato and
Arugula Salad, 148
Sun-Dried Tomatoes, 285
Tortilla of Cast-Iron Fried Potatoes,
Spinach, and Sun-Dried
Tomatoes, 65
Tortilla of Cast-Iron Fried Potatoes,
Spinach, and Sun-Dried
Tomatoes, 65
Tortilla of Prawns with Grilled Potatoes
and Avocado, Chile Pepper, and
Fennel Salsa, 69
tuna, Churrasco of Tuna with Coal-
Burnt Pimentón Oil, Heirloom
Tomato and Chard Salad, and
Garlicky Potato Puree, 170–71
Tuna Churrasco and Avocado
Sandwich, 78
Tuna Tartare with Crunchy Bread
Crumbs, 47
turnips, Baby Turnips a la Plancha
with Sun-Dried Tomatoes, 208

umbilicus, 30
Uruguay, 163–64

veal:
Calves' Liver a la Plancha with
Pimentón Oil, Onions, and
Crunchy Potatoes, 105
Sliced Kidney Strips a la Plancha
with Salsa Provenzal, 104
Veal Rib Chops and French Green
Beans a la Plancha with

Romaine-Watercress Salad, 93
vegetables:
fire cooking and, 18, 116, 119, 152
Parrillada of Pork and Vegetables,
116–21
Rich Vegetable Stock, 288
see also specific vegetables
Vergé, Roger, 57
vinegar:
Duck Breast with Balsamic Vinegar
and Asparagus, 158
Grilled Short Ribs with Vinegar-
Glazed Charred Endive, 101

walnuts, Endive Salad with Mustard,
Aged Goat Cheese, and Toasted
Walnuts, 52
Walton, Izaak, 181
watercress:
Grilled Skirt Steak Sandwich with
Watercress, Onion, Tomato, and
Mustard, 76
Veal Rib Chops and French
Green Beans a la Plancha with
Romaine-Watercress Salad, 93
Waters, Alice, 52, 176
Weeping Lamb, 108
wine:
Braised Beans with Red Wine and
Tomato, 215
Mussels Steamed in Red Wine-
Butter Sauce with Shallots and
Parsley, 201
Pressed Pears and Plums in Red
Wine with Rosemary, 258
Red-Wine-Braised Spareribs with
Red Cabbage and Carrot Slaw,
133

yogurt, Prawns, Sardines, and
Anchovies a la Plancha with
Zucchini, Swiss Chard, and
Minted Yogurt, 196

zucchini:
Coal-Roasted Zucchini and Swiss
Chard, 223
Huevos Escrachados with
Pancetta, Zucchini Ribbons, and
Green Peas, 64
Prawns, Sardines, and Anchovies
a la Plancha with Zucchini, Swiss
Chard, and Minted Yogurt, 196

PHOTO CREDITS

Santiago Soto Monllor: pages viii, x–xi, xii (both), xiii (right), xiv, 4–5, 6, 9, 12, 14 (both), 15 (both), 16, 19, 20, 23, 24, 27, 28, 29 (both), 31, 32, 34 (both), 35, 37, 38 (both), 42, 43, 46, 47, 48, 51, 53, 54, 55, 56–57, 59 (all), 60, 62, 66 (both), 67 (both), 68, 70–71, 73, 74, 77, 80, 82, 83, 84–85, 87 (all), 88–89, 90, 92, 95, 96, 99, 100, 103, 106, 107, 110–11 (both), 113 (both), 114, 117, 118 (right), 126, 127, 130 (both), 131, 132, 134, 135, 136, 137, 139, 140–41, 143 (all), 144, 146 (both), 147, 150, 151 (both), 153, 154–55, 155 (right), 156, 159, 160, 161, 162–63, 165 (top center, middle row left and center, bottom three), 166–67, 171, 172, 173, 175, 177, 178–79, 180, 182–83 (all), 184, 186, 187 (both), 189, 194, 195 (both), 198–99 (both), 202, 206, 209 (both), 210–11, 212, 217 (both), 218 (both), 221, 224, 225, 227, 230 (both), 231 (both), 240, 242, 245, 247, 248, 250 (both), 252–53 (both), 255, 256 (both), 257, 260 (both), 261 (both), 262, 264 (both), 269, 270, 271, 275 (middle row left and right, bottom row center), 276, 280, 282, 286, 288, 291, and 293 (all except bottom row center).

Quentin Bacon: pages 118 (left), 123, 293 (bottom row center), and 295.

Nate Bressler: pages iv–v, 272–73, 275 (top row right, middle row center), and 277.

Peter Buchanan-Smith: 275 (top row left and center, middle row center), and 306.

Nicolás Colledani: pages 190–91 (both).

Eugenia Daneri (courtesy of *Para Ti Deco*): pages xiii (center), 165 (top left and right, middle row right, bottom row center), and 246.

Estudio Garcia Betancourt: pages vi-vii.

Michael Evans: pages ii–iii, xiii (left), 138, and 294.

Tom Wesley: pages 10–11, and 110 (left).

Eric Wolfinger: pages 40–41, 50, 168, 205, 222, 232, 233, 234–35, 237 (all), 238, 239, and 278.

CONVERSION TABLES

Here are rounded-off equivalents between the metric system and the traditional systems that are used in the United States to measure weight and volume.

WEIGHTS

US/UK	Metric
¼ oz	7 g
½ oz	15 g
1 oz	30 g
2 oz	55 g
3 oz	85 g
4 oz	110 g
5 oz	140 g
6 oz	170 g
7 oz	200 g
8 oz (½ lb)	225 g
9 oz	250 g
10 oz	280 g
11 oz	310 g
12 oz	340 g
13 oz	370 g
14 oz	400 g
15 oz	425 g
16 oz (1 lb)	450 g

VOLUME

American	Imperial	Metric
¼ tsp		1.25 ml
½ tsp		2.5 ml
1 tsp		5 ml
½ Tbs (1½ tsp)		7.5 ml
1 Tbs (3 tsp)		15 ml
¼ cup (4 Tbs)	2 fl oz	60 ml
⅓ cup (5 Tbs)	2½ fl oz	75 ml
½ cup (8 Tbs)	4 fl oz	125 ml
⅔ cup (10 Tbs)	5 fl oz	150 ml
¾ cup (12 Tbs)	6 fl oz	175 ml
1 cup (16 Tbs)	8 fl oz	250 ml
1¼ cups	10 fl oz	300 ml
1½ cups	12 fl oz	350 ml
1 pint (2 cups)	16 fl oz	500 ml
2½ cups	20 fl oz (1 pint)	625 ml
5 cups	40 fl oz (1 qt)	1.25 l

OVEN TEMPERATURES

	°F	°C	Gas Mark
very cool	250–275	130–140	½–1
cool	300	148	2
warm	325	163	3
moderate	350	177	4
moderately hot	375–400	190–204	5–6
hot	425	218	7
very hot	450–475	232–245	8–9

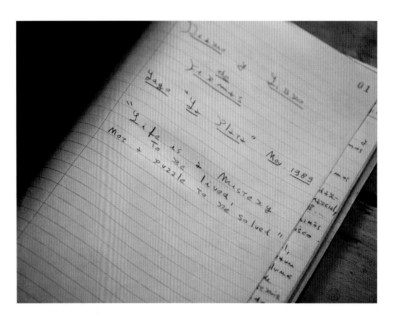

The only things I ask of my guests at "The Island" are that they bring a favorite book for the library, sign this guest book, and leave the world behind.